AF522609

HIGHER EDUCATION AFTER GLOBALISATION

HIGHER EDUCATION AFTER GLOBALISATION

Edited by

Dr. Rabi Narayana Misra

M.com., LL.B., M.Phil, Ph.D.

Professor

Dept. of MBA, SMIT, Berhampur

Biju Patnaik University & Technology (BPUT)

(Orissa) (India)

DISCOVERY PUBLISHING HOUSE PVT. LTD.

NEW DELHI-110 002

Published by:
Tilak Wasan

DISCOVERY PUBLISHING HOUSE PVT. LTD.
4383/4B, Ansari Road, Darya Ganj
New Delhi-110 002 (India)
Phone : +91-11-23279245, 43596064-65
Fax : +91-11-23253475
E-mail : discoverypublishinghouse@gmail.com
sales@discoverypublishinggroup.com
parul.wasan@gmail.com
web : www.discoverypublishinggroup.com

First Edition: **2014**

ISBN: 978-93-5056-440-0

Higher Education after Globalisation

Printed at:
Dynamic Printers
Delhi

Preface

Education has made a significant contribution in economic development, social progress and political democracy in independent India. Good education system develops human resources of employees working in the organization. The study of human resources development in our country is vital from the point of view of overall economic welfare.

Education tends to emphasize individual achievement and personal importance which may run towards the quality circle progress. Higher education in India faces serious challenges and it needs a systematic overhaul, so that more and more people educated at colleges and universities level. Quality education is to be taken into due consideration after globalisation. The present higher education system needs meaningful reforms to increase quality knowledge in the mind of the persons who are working in the different fields. To meet the challenges after globalisation higher education is considered as an important tool for the growth and development of human skill for proper utilisation of same for overall development of the country.

Author

Acknowledgements

I am very much thankful to all paper contributors of this book. It is not possible in my part to edit this book without their help and co-operation.

I am also thankful to my wife Smt. Swarna Prava Misra for her timely help and co-operation for editing this book. My sons Roopesh and Rookesh have provided their helping hands in editing this book, so I am also thankful to them. My elder daughter-in-law Smt. Amrita Rani Misra and younger daughter-in-law Smt. Bandita Misra have also given their timely help in editing this book.

My special thanks to Mr. Tilak Wasan, the Owner/Director of Discovery Publishing House (P) Ltd., New Delhi for publishing this book in time. I have also provided my thanks to his son who is the real leader in publishing this book. At last I would like to thanks all members of publishing division of Discovery Publishing House for help and co-operation in publishing this book in time.

Author

Contents

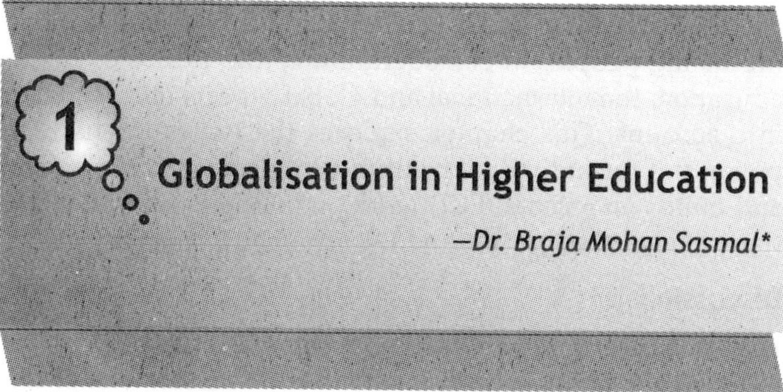

1 Globalisation in Higher Education

*—Dr. Braja Mohan Sasmal**

Introduction

The notion of globalisation was actually launched towards the end of twentieth century as a result of rapid advancement in the fields of Science and Technology throughout the world. Globalisation is a modern scientific process or method, by which all nations of the world are inter-connected with an aim to centrally develop social, economic and cultural conditions of the people living there in and for promotion of international relationship among the nations. In global knowledge economics, higher education institutions are more important than ever as mediums for a wide range of cross-border relationships and continuous global flows of people, information, knowledge, technologies, products and financial capital. 'Not all universities are (particularly) international, but all are subject to the same processes of globalisation - partly as objects, victims even, of these processes, but partly as subjects, or key agents, of globalisation. Even as they share in the reinvention of the world around them, higher education institutions and the policies that produce and support them, are also being reinvented.

In the present era of Super Computers and modern internet systems, higher education plays an important role in

*Professor, Brahmapur (Gm), Odisha.

the development of social, economic, cultural and educational life of the people. In consideration of the future of higher education, the international and global aspects must be taken into account. This chapter explores the issues for national policy and for individual institution. As such it complements and builds on recent OECD work on Internationalisation and trade in higher education and E-learning in tertiary education.

Discussion

Higher education is always more internationally open than most sectors because of its involvement with knowledge and wisdom of the people. Therefore, higher education now becomes central to the changes sweeping through world wide network communications, which are reshaping the social, economic and cultural conditions of the people. In recent years, higher education institutions and their policies throughout the world are being reoriented under the advanced guidelines of globalisation process. Presently, globalisation is widening, depending and speeding up the international relationship, higher education policies and its systems among the nations of the world.

A generation ago, international relations were largely marginal to the day-to-day operations of institutions and systems, except in scientific research. Now, the growing impact of the global environment is in-escapable. In many nations international mobility, global comparison, bench-making, ranking and Intel-nationalisation of the higher educational institutions and their systems are the key policy themes.

In this era globalisation combines economic and cultural change. On one hand globalisation entails the formation of world-wide markets operating in real time in common financial systems, and unprecedented levels of foreign direct investment and cross-border mobility of production. On the other hand it rests on the first world-wide systems of communications, information, education and culture, tending towards a single world community as Marshall McLuhan (1964) predicted. Continuously extending networks based on travel, mobile phones, broad-band Internet and other information and communications technologies (ICTs), are creating new forms of inter-subjective human association, of unprecedented scale and flexibility; Spanning cities and nations with varied cultures and levels of economic development and enable the complex data transfers essential to knowledge-intensive production. It is the processes of communications and information, where the economic and cultural aspects are drawn together, that above all constitutes what is new about globalisation; and inclusion/exclusion in relation to ICT networks and Higher Education have become key dividing line in shaping relations of power and inequality.

Higher education is implicated in all these changes. Education and research are key elements in the formation of the global environment, being foundational to knowledge, the take-up of technologies, cross-border association and sustaining complex communities. Though higher education institutions often see themselves as objects of globalisation they are also its agents (Scott, 1988). Research universities are intensively linked within and between the global cities that constitute the major nodes of a networked world. Characteristically global cities have a high density of participation in ratio of a nation or a region, and its global competitive performance. Correspondingly, nations and regions that are relatively decoupled from the globally networked economy are typified by a low density of higher education.

For certain higher education operations have become the primary English speaking nations, international operations have become the primary mode of development. In Europe, the negotiation of the common higher education area and the European research area have been made explicit the processes where by a large section of global higher education environment is being formed.

At the same time, globalisation is not a single universal phenomenon. It is functioning according to local situations, language of use, academic cultures and it plays out very differently according to the types of Higher Educational institutions. In a networked global environment in which every university of the global dimension is increasing day-by-day. It is no longer possible for individual nation or for individual higher education institution to completely seal themselves off from global effects. But, research intensive universities and smaller number of vocational universities, organized as global international business, tends to be the most implicated globalisation. Typically, they are more internationally networked than the bulk of the societies in which they are situated. Research intensive universities, that down play global connectivity, pay the price in diminished effectiveness.

On the other hand with some exceptions predominantly teaching institutions, community colleges and traditional vocational sectors are less engaged and effected. Likewise globalisation does not take place on a level playing field. Nations and institutions bring varying capacities and agendas to global exchange. Cross border flows between nations are not symmetrical. Nor is every national system, engaged with every other to the same extent or intensity. For example the higher educational institutions of United States exercise a profound global influence; yet in some ways seem less effected than others. Globalisation can also vary according to policy, governance and management of higher educational institutions: Nations and institutions have space in which to pilot their own global engagements. But this self- determination, operates within limits, that constrain some nations and institutions more than others. In consideration of the future of higher education, the international and global aspects must be taken into account. Globalisation of higher education explores the issues for national policy and for individual institution. As such it complements and builds on recent OECD work on inter-nationalisation and trade in higher education and E-learning in tertiary education.

Being deeply immersed in global transformation, higher education is itself being transformed on both sides of the economy/culture symbiosis. Higher education is swept up in global marketisation. It trains the executives and technicians of global businesses; the main student growth is in globally mobile degrees in business studies and computing; the sector is shaped by economic policies undergoing partial global convergence, and the first global university market has emerged. Even larger changes are happening on the cultural side. Teichler (2004) remarks that 'it is surprising to note how much the debate on global phenomena in higher education suddenly focuses on marketisation, competition and management in higher education.' Other terms, such as knowledge or education society, global village, global understanding or global learning are hardly taken into consideration. It is surprising because while higher education is a second level player in the circuits of capital and direct creation of economic wealth, it is pivotal to research and knowledge, constitutive in language, information and cross-cultural encounters, and has many connections with media and communication. Information and knowledge are highly mobile readily slipping across borders, so that the cultural sphere of higher education, in which research and information are produced, is actually more globalised than the economic sphere. Above all there is the ever-extending Internet, supporting intellectual goods whose use value far exceeds the cost of their distribution and consumption. Advanced higher education is now unimaginable without it. The size, speed and complexity of information increasingly penetrate the daily live of scientists. The Internet facilitates world-wide databases and collaboration between academic faculty, stimulating more face-to face and electronic meetings. Cross-border e-learning, combining ICTs and teaching has not displaced existing educational institutions as some expected but continues to grow, with open potential for new kinds of pedagogy and access.

Conclusion

The entire discussions so far carried out on the subject-matter may be concluded finally as follows:

1. It provides an overall discussion on globalisation in higher education and global responses of national systems and policies of higher education.
2. It discusses the factors responsible for shaping policy, interpretations of globalisation and argues for a neutral approach to its' true definitions.
3. It summarises the global strategic environment and variations between national higher education systems and institutions in experiences of globalisation.
4. It also draws out the meta-policy implications of Globalisation in partial dis-embending of intuitions from their national contexts and the growing role of global public and private goods in higher education and research.
5. It viewed on national policy implications of globalisation, particularly in three major areas of higher education, these are research intensive universities, the cross border markets in vocational degree level institutions and non-university institutions.
6. It also focused on certain areas of National Education Policy with a strong multilateral dimensions; such as Europeonisation of education systems, institutional ranking and typologies and cross border mobility.
7. Finally, it may be concluded that the entire globalisation process is for boosting the quality of higher educational institutions in developed nations, but it is partially successful in under-developed nations due to the various reasons including the brain drain issues and cross border issues.

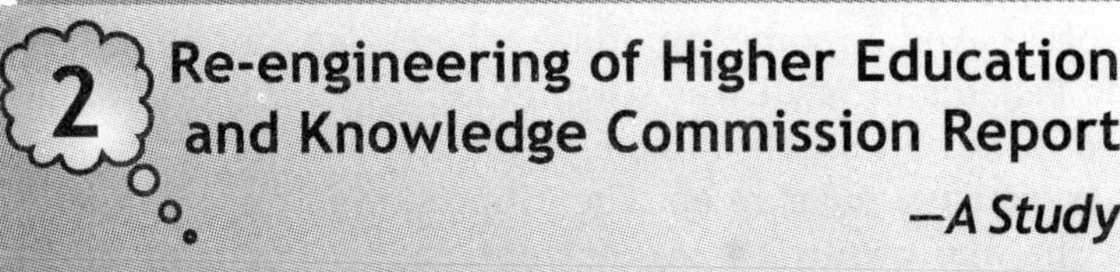

2 Re-engineering of Higher Education and Knowledge Commission Report —*A Study*

*—Dr. H. Srinivasa Rao**

*—Dr. R.N. Misra***

Introduction

The spread of education in society is at the foundation of success in countries that are late-comers to development. In the quest for development, primary education is absolutely essential because it creates the base. But higher education is just as important, for it provides the cutting edge and universities are the life-blood of higher education. Islands of excellence in professional education, such as IITs and IIMs, are valuable complements but cannot be substitutes for universities which provide educational opportunities for people at large.

There can be no doubt that higher education has made a significant contribution to economic development, social progress and political democracy in independent India. It is a source of dynamism for the economy. It has created social opportunities for people. It has fostered the vibrant democracy in our polity. It has provided a beginning for the creation of a knowledge society. But it would be a mistake to focus on its strengths alone. It has weaknesses that are a cause for serious concern.

There is, in fact, a quiet crisis in higher education in India that runs deep. It is not yet discernible simply because there

*Reader in Commerce, Badurka College of Commerce, Hyderabad, A.P.
**Professor of MBA, S.M.I.T., Berhampur, Orissa.

are pockets of excellence, an enormous reservoir of talented young people and an intense competition in the admissions process. And, in some important spheres, we continue to reap the benefits of what was sown in higher education 50 years ago by the founding fathers of the Republic. The reality is that we have miles to go. The proportion of our population, in the age group 18-24, that enters the world of higher education is around 7 per cent, which is only one-half the average for Asia. The opportunities for higher education, in terms of the number of places in universities, are simply not enough in relation to our needs. What is more, the quality of higher education in most of our universities requires substantial improvement.

It is clear that the system of higher education in India faces serious challenges. And it needs a systematic overhaul, so that we can educate much larger numbers without diluting academic standards. This is imperative because the transformation of economy and society in the twenty-first century would depend, in significant part, on the spread and the quality of education among our people, particularly in the sphere of higher education, It is only an inclusive society that can provide the foundations for a knowledge society.

The challenges that confront higher education in India are clear. It needs a massive expansion of opportunities for higher education, to 1500 universities nationwide, that would enable India to attain a gross enrolment ratio of at least 15 per cent by 2015. It is just as important to raise the average quality of higher education in every sphere. At the same time, it is essential to create institutions that are exemplars of excellence at par with the best in the world. In the pursuit of these objectives, providing people with access to higher education in a socially inclusive manner is imperative. The realization of these objectives, combined with access, would not only develop the skills and capabilities we need for the economy but would also help transform India into a knowledge economy and society.

We recognise that a meaningful reform of the higher education system, with a long-term perspective is both complex and difficult Yet, it is imperative. We would suggest the following building blocks in this endeavour. First, it is essential to reform existing public universities and undergraduate colleges. Second, it is necessary to overhaul the entire regulatory structure governing higher education. Third, every possible source of financing investment in higher education needs to be explored. Fourth, it is important to think about pro-active strategies for enhancement of quality in higher education. Fifth, the time has come to create new institutions in the form of National Universities that would become role models as centres of academic excellence. Sixth, the higher education system must be so designed that it provides access to marginalized and excluded groups.

Universities

Universities perform a critical role in an economy and society. They create knowledge. They impart knowledge. And they disseminate knowledge. Universities must be flexible, innovative and creative. They must be able to attract the best talent whether teachers or students. They must have the ability to compete and the motivation to excel. We cannot even contemplate a transformation of our higher education system without reform in our existing universities.

There is, however, a serious cause for concern about universities in India. The number of places for students at universities is simply inadequate. The quality of education at most universities leaves much to be desired. The gap between our universities and those in the outside world has widened. And none of our universities rank among the best, say the top fifty, in the world. The symptoms are clearly visible, even if we do not wish to diagnose what ails our universities. Of course, every problem does not exist everywhere. And there are exceptions. But the following problems are common enough to be a cause for concern. First, curricula, which have remained almost unchanged for decades, have not kept pace with the times, let alone with the extending frontiers of knowledge. Second, learning and creativity are at a discount in a system of assessment that places a premium on memory rather than understanding. Third, the milieu is not conducive to anything beyond the class room, for it is caught in a 9.30 to 1.30 syndrome. Fourth, the academic calendar is no longer sacrosanct for classes or for examinations, as there are slippages in schedules so much so that, at several places, classes in the time-table are not held and results are often declared with a time-lag of 6 to 12 months. Fifth, the infrastructure is not only inadequate but also on the verge of collapse. Sixth, the boundaries between disciplines have become dividing walls that constitute barriers to entry for new disciplines or new courses, while knowledge is developing most rapidly at the inter-section of disciplines. Seventh, the importance attached to research has eroded steadily over time. Eighth, the volume of research in terms of frequency of publication and the quality of research reflected in the frequency of citation or the place of publication, on balance, is simply not what it used to be. Ninth, as in most public institutions, there is little accountability, because there are no rewards for performance and no penalties for non-performance. Tenth, structures of governance put in place fifty years ago are not responsive to changing times and circumstances but the system is readily subverted by vested interests.

It is difficult enough to provide a complete diagnosis of what ails our universities. It is even more difficult, if not impossible, to outline a set of prescriptions for our universities. Nevertheless, it is clear that a reform of existing institutions must be an integral part of our endeavour to transform higher education. We recognise that this is easier said than done. Even so, we believe that reforms in the following spheres, along the lines suggested by us, are not only possible but would also make a difference.

Number and Size

India has about 350 universities. This number is simply not enough with reference to our needs in higher education, or in comparison with China which has authorised the creation of 1250 new universities in the past three years. Yet, some of our universities are much too large, for ensuring academic standards and providing good governance. We need to create more appropriately scaled and more nimble universities. The moral of the story is not only that we need a much larger number of universities, say 1500 nationwide by 2015, but also that we need smaller universities which are responsive to change and easier to manage.

Curriculum

The syllabi of courses in universities, which remain unchanged for decades, need to be upgraded constantly and revised frequently. The laws of inertia reinforced by resistance to change must be overcome. Universities should be required to revise or restructure curricula at least once in three years. These revisions must be subjected to outside peer review before implementation. The process for such revisions should be streamlined and decentralised, with more autonomy for teachers, through a change in statutes wherever necessary. For existing systems often act as major impediments to a timely or speedy revision of curricula. There should be some mode of censure for departments or universities that do not upgrade their courses regularly. It needs to be recognised that it is very difficult to introduce new courses or innovative courses in universities because of departmental divides. Appropriate institutional mechanisms should be put in place to resolve this problem.

Assessment

The nature of annual examinations at universities in India often stifles the teaching-learning process because they reward selective and uncritical learning. There is an acute need to reform this examination system so that it tests understanding rather than memory. Analytical abilities and creative thinking should be at a premium. Learning by rote should be at a discount. Such reform would become more feasible with decentralised examination and smaller universities. But assessment cannot and should not be based on examinations alone. There is a clear need for continuous internal assessment which empowers teachers and students alike, just as it breathes life back into the teaching-learning process. Such internal assessment would also foster the analytical and creative abilities of students which are often a casualty in university-administered annual examinations. To begin with, internal assessment could have a weight of 25 per cent in the total but this should be raised to 50 per cent over time.

Course Credits

The present system is characterised by too many rigidities and too few choices for students. Universities that are smaller, or run semester-based systems, are obviously more flexible. Even in large universities, however, it is necessary to introduce greater diversity and more flexibility in course structures. This would be the beginning of a transition to a course credit system, where degrees are granted on the basis of completing a requisite number of credits from different courses. Every student should be required to earn a minimum number of credits in his/her chosen discipline but should have the freedom to earn the rest from courses in other disciplines. It is essential to provide students with choices instead of keeping them captive.

Research

We attempted to create stand-alone research institutions, pampered with resources, in the belief that research should be moved out of universities. In the process, we forgot an essential principle. There are synergies between teaching and research that enrich each other. And it is universities which are the natural home for research. What is more, for universities, research is essential in the pursuit of academic excellence. It is time to reverse what happened in the past and make universities the hub of research once again. This would need changes in resource-allocation, reward-systems and mind-sets. Substantial grants should be allocated for research. The provisions of these grants should be competitive and the criteria for these grants should be different from the usual criteria for non-plan and plan grants.

Faculty

There must be a conscious effort to attract and retain talented faculty members. This is necessary because talented students who are potential faculty members have choices that are far more attractive in other professions in India or in the academic profession outside India. It is necessary to provide working conditions in the form of office space and research support combined with housing. But it may not be sufficient. This must be combined with some incentives and rewards for performance. There is, however, another dimension to the problem. Universities do not always choose the best in part because of native-son/daughter policies which leave them to select their own former students. This tends to lower quality and foster parochialisation in universities. Therefore, cross-pollination between universities should be encouraged. It may be worth introducing a ceiling, say one-half or even one-third, on the proportion of faculty members than can be hired from within the university. This would almost certainly engender greater competition and more transparency in faculty appointments.

Finances

There is a serious resource crunch in universities which leaves them with little financial flexibility. In general, about 75 per cent of maintenance expenditure is on salaries and pensions. Of the remaining 25 per cent, at least 15 per cent is absorbed by pre-emptive claims such as rents, electricity, telephones and examinations. The balance, less than 10 per cent, is not even enough for maintenance let alone development.

Laboratories and libraries languish while buildings crumble. But that is not all. In most universities, plan (investment) expenditure is less than 5 per cent of non-plan (maintenance) expenditure. Such a small proportion of investment in total expenditure can only mortgage the future. It is doing so. The time has come for some strategic thinking on the re-allocation of budgets for universities with some allocation for development grants and on needs other than salaries. The criteria for resource allocation should seek to strike a much better balance between providing for salaries/pensions and providing for maintenance/development/investment. These criteria should recognise the importance of a critical minimum to ensure standards and strategic preferences to promote excellence.

Infrastructure

The elements of infrastructure that support the teaching-learning process, most directly, need to be monitored and upgraded on a regular basis. This means attention particular attention to libraries and laboratories, in addition to class rooms, sports facilities and auditoria. It is imperative that universities provide broadband and connectivity to all students and teachers in campuses. In parallel, information technology systems should be used for admissions, administration and examinations along with other relevant web services for campus communities. And, as soon as possible, a digital infrastructure for networking universities should be put in place.

Governance

There is an acute need for reform in the structures of governance of universities. The present system is flawed. On the one hand, it does not preserve autonomy. On the other, it does not promote accountability. The autonomy of universities is eroded by interventions from governments and intrusions from political processes. This must be stopped. At the same time, there is not enough transparency and accountability in universities. This must be fostered. It is exceedingly difficult to provide generalised prescriptions. Some steps, which would constitute an important beginning, are clear. First, the appointments of Vice-Chancellors should be based on search processes and peer judgement alone. These must be freed from direct or indirect intervention on the part of governments. Once appointed, Vice-Chancellors should have a tenure of six years, because the existing tenure of three years in most universities and five years in Central Universities is not long enough. Second, the size and composition of University Courts, Academic Councils and Executive Councils slows down decision-making processes and sometimes constitutes an impediment to change. University Courts, with a size of 500 plus, which are more a ritual than substance, could be dispensed with. Large Academic Councils do not meet often. Even when they meet, decisions are slow to come. Thus, Standing Committees of Academic Councils, which are representative, should be created for frequent meetings and expeditious decisions. The Vice-Chancellor should, then, function as a Chief Executive Officer who has the authority and the flexibility to govern with the advice and consent of the Executive Council which would provide checks and balances to create accountability. Third, experience suggests that implicit politicisation has made governance of universities exceedingly difficult and much more susceptible to entirely non-academic interventions from outside. This problem needs to be recognised and addressed in a systematic manner not only within universities but also outside, particularly in governments, legislatures and political parties.

Undergraduate Colleges

Undergraduate education, which accounts for about 85 per cent of the enrolled students, is the largest component of our higher education system. It is imparted through colleges where students enrol for first degrees in Arts, Science or Commerce. There are a total of about 17,700 undergraduate colleges. Of these, a mere 200 colleges are autonomous. The rest, as many as 17,500 colleges, are affiliated to, or constituent in, 131 universities. On average, each university has more than 100 affiliated colleges, but there are some universities each of which has more than 400 affiliated colleges.

This system of affiliated colleges for undergraduate education, which may have been appropriate fifty years ago, is neither adequate nor appropriate at this juncture, let alone for the future. It is cumbersome to manage. And it is difficult to ensure minimal academic standards across the board. The problem has at least three dimensions. First, it imposes an onerous burden on universities which have to regulate admissions, set curricula and conduct examinations for such a large number of undergraduate colleges. The problem is compounded by uneven standards and geographical dispersion. Second, the undergraduate colleges are constrained by their affiliated status, in terms of autonomy and space, which makes it difficult for them to adapt, to innovate and to evolve. The problem is particularly acute for undergraduate colleges that are good, for both teachers and students are subjected to the 'convoy problem' insofar as they are forced to move at the speed of the slowest. There is also a problem for undergraduate colleges that are not so good, or are poor, because universities cannot address their special needs or unique problems. Third, it is difficult to set curricula and assess performance for such a large number of students where there is such a large dispersion in performance at school before entering college. This reality tends to make courses less demanding and examinations less stringent across the board. In fact the design of courses and examinations needs to be flexible rather than exactly the same for large student communities.

There is an urgent need to restructure the system of undergraduate colleges affiliated to universities. In doing so, it is important to make a distinction between undergraduate colleges that already exist and undergraduate colleges that will be established in the future. It is also important to remember that undergraduate colleges are afflicted by problems which are very similar to those that afflict universities.

The most obvious solution is to provide autonomy to colleges, either as individual colleges or as clusters of colleges.

Individual Colleges

Colleges with a proven record of academic excellence and efficient administrative functioning can be granted autonomy in terms of academic self-governance. Existing affiliated or constituent colleges should be granted autonomy in phases after due assessment by professional accreditation bodies. A review of performance of these colleges should be institutionalised and they may be granted university status on the fulfilment of stated criteria of academic and administrative performance. The college authorities should be given financial autonomy with regard to internal allocation of resources. However existing methods of financing should be retained. In operational terms, then, the autonomy would be accorded in setting of curriculum and evaluation of students.

College Clusters

Autonomy can be provided to clusters of colleges, selected on the basis of criteria such as similar standards or geographical proximity. These colleges could then form a group, complementing each other, offering different courses between them. In time, these clusters could be upgraded to universities. The course-credit system can be implemented in these autonomous clusters, whereby different colleges offer semester-based courses on a credit system and credits can be transferred across colleges. A mechanism for the administration of courses across colleges and for the resolution of problems should be institutionalized with provision for representation in committees.

Such autonomous colleges, or clusters of colleges, would constitute a part of the 1500 universities we propose nation-wide by 2015. It must be recognised, however, that this is, at best, a limited solution. There are two discernible problems.

The first problem with the model of autonomous colleges is the principal-agent problem of providing autonomy as an option. It becomes necessary to distinguish between the motivations and the capabilities of colleges. We need to make a distinction between colleges that wish to become autonomous but do not deserve to, and colleges that have the capabilities to be autonomous but do not wish to opt for autonomy. For colleges that wish to become autonomous but may not be suitable, clear cut criteria should be put in place as a filtering mechanism for colleges wishing to attain autonomous status: critical number of faculty and disciplines, governance, track record in terms of students, faculty and research, administrative competence measured by utilization of grants, regularity of audits, office resources and account maintenance, contribution to university processes, infrastructural facilities and ratings, if available, by accreditation agencies. For colleges that can be autonomous but do not wish to be, appropriate incentives have to be designed, especially for the teaching staff to encourage a move towards autonomy. Institutional incentives relating to funding and resource generation and professional incentives for staff including positions of professors, research grants and greater mobility should be provided.

The second problem with the model of autonomous colleges is that it would be able to provide a solution for a limited proportion, or number, of undergraduate colleges. There would be a significant number of undergraduate colleges that would remain because they may not have the capabilities to become autonomous or join an autonomous cluster. The obvious solution would be for this latter group to continue as affiliated colleges with their present universities. In that event, problems will persist not only for these undergraduate colleges but also for their affiliating universities. Nevertheless, a proportion of these undergraduate colleges will continue to be affiliated to their present universities on the basis of stipulated criteria. There are two other possibilities that could be explored.

The first possibility is that some of these affiliated colleges could be remodelled as community colleges. These colleges could provide both vocational education through two-year courses and formal education through three-year courses. This would serve the needs of a particular segment of the student population better. They could focus on promoting job-oriented, work-related, skill-based and life-coping education. These community colleges could provide a unique opportunity to provide holistic education and eligibility for employment to the disadvantage.

The second possibility is that we establish a Central Board of Undergraduate Education along with State Boards of Undergraduate Education which would set curricula and conduct examinations for undergraduate colleges that choose to be affiliated with them. These Boards would separate the academic functions from the administrative functions and at the sàme time provide quality benchmarks. Governance would become much simpler. It is possible mat some of the existing undergraduate colleges, particularly those that are at some geographical distance from their parent university, may wish to affiliate themselves to these Boards.

New undergraduate colleges are bound to be an integral part of the expansion of opportunities in higher education. Where would these be located? It would be difficult for them to become autonomous colleges without a track record. It may be possible for some to join a cluster of autonomous colleges but this would be more the exception than the rule. It would not be possible for them to affiliate with existing universities which are already overloaded. Hence, there are three possible options for new undergraduate colleges to come. First, they could be established as community colleges. Second, they could be affiliated with the Central Board of Undergraduate Education or State Boards of Undergraduate Education. Third, they could be affiliated with new universities that are established.

There are, of course, issues related to governance, curricula, examinations, course credits and access which arise in the context of undergraduate colleges. These have been discussed in the context of universities in the preceding section of this note.

Regulation

There is a clear need to establish an Independent Regulatory Authority for Higher Education (IRAHE). Such a regulatory authority is both necessary and desirable.

It is necessary for two important reasons. First, in India, it requires an Act of Legislature of Parliament to set up a University. The deemed university route is much top difficult for new institutions. Entry through legislation alone, as at present, is a formidable barrier. The consequence is a steady increase in the average size of existing universities with a steady deterioration in their quality. The absence of competition only compounds problems. Second, as we seek to expand the higher education system, entry norms will be needed for private institutions and public-private partnerships. The institutional framework for this purpose must be put in place here and now.

It is desirable for four important reasons. First, it would minimise conflicts of interest as it would create an arm's-length distance from stakeholders. Second, it would replace the present system which is over-regulated but under-governed, through more appropriate forms of intervention. Third, it would rationalize the existing system where mandates are both confusing and overlapping. Fourth, it would dispense with the multiplicity of regulatory agencies to provide a single-window clearance.

The present regulatory system in higher education is flawed in many respects. The barriers to entry are too high. The system of authorizing entry is cumbersome. And there are extensive rules after entry, as the UGC seeks to regulate almost every aspect of an institution from fees to curriculum. The system is also based on patently irrational, principles.

Section 3.1.2(*a*) of the UGC Act suggests that permission for receiving grants will be accorded only if the Commission is satisfied that the existing institutions in the state are not adequate to serve the needs of the state. The other regulators, say in the sphere of professional education, are often inconsistent in their adherence to principles. There are several instances where an engineering college or a business school is approved, promptly, in a small house of a metropolitan suburb without the requisite teachers, infrastructure or facilities, but established universities experience difficulties in obtaining similar approvals. Such examples can be multiplied. These would only confirm that the complexity, the multiplicity and the rigidity of the existing regulatory structure is not conducive to the expansion of higher education opportunities in India.

In sum, the existing regulatory framework constrains the supply of good institutions, excessively regulates existing institutions in the wrong places, and is not conducive to innovation or creativity in higher education. The challenge is therefore to design a regulatory system that increases the supply of good institutions and fosters accountability in those institutions. An independent regulator has to be the cornerstone of such a system.

The proposed IRAHE will rationalize the principles on which entry is regulated. There are two aspects to this rationalization: what is to be regulated and what are the principles used for regulation.

In higher education, regulators perform five functions: (1) Entry: licence to grant degrees. (2) Accreditation: quality benchmarking. (3) Disbursement of public funds. (4) Access: fees or affirmative action. (5) Licence: to practice profession.

India is perhaps the only country in the world where regulation in 4 of the 5 functions is carried out by one entity, that is, the UGC. The purpose of creating an IRAHE is to separate these functions. The proposed IRAHE shall be responsible for setting the criteria and deciding on entry. It would, in addition, license agencies to take care of accreditation. The role of the UGC will be limited to disbursing public funds. Issues of access will be governed by state legislation on reservations and other forms of affirmative action. And, professional associations may, in some institutions, set requirements to determine eligibility for conducting a profession. All other regulatory agencies such as the AICTE will need to be abolished while the MCI and the BCI will be limited to their role as professional associations. These professional associations could conduct nationwide examinations to provide licences for those wishing to enter the profession.

The second aspect of regulation is the principle used to regulate. The IRAHE will determine eligibility for setting up a new institution based on transparent criteria rather than discretionary controls. Its main role would be to exercise due diligence at the point it approves a licence to grant degrees. In doing so, it would assess the academic credibility and the financial viability of the proposed institution on the basis of information submitted in accordance with the stipulated criteria. It will apply exactly the same norms to public and private institutions, just as it will apply the same norms to domestic and international institutions.

The IRAHE would be constituted as follows. It would have a Chairperson and six members. The tenure of the Chairperson would be six years. The tenure of the members would also be six years. One-third of the members of the Authority will retire every two years. The Chairperson would be a distinguished academic from any discipline with experience of governance in higher education. The members would be distinguished academics drawn from the following sets of disciplines; physical sciences, life sciences, social sciences, humanities and professional subjects such as engineering, medicine, law or management. The IRAHE could have some part-time members or standing committees drawn from academia to advise the Authority in each of the aforesaid sets of disciplines. The Chairperson and the Members of the

IRAHE would be appointed by the Prime Minister based on the recommendations of a Search Committee.

The IRAHE would have to be established by an Act of Parliament. It would be the only agency that would be authorised to accord degree granting power to higher education institutions. It would also be responsible for monitoring standards and settling disputes. It should also be thought of as the authority for licensing accreditation agencies. The IRAHE must be at an arm's-length from the government and independent of all stakeholders including the concerned Ministries of the Government. The Acts of the UGC, AICTE, MCI and BCI would have to be amended. The role of the UGC would be re-defined to focus on the disbursement of grants to, and maintenance of, public institutions in higher education. The entry regulatory functions of the AICTE, the MCI and the BCI would be performed by the IRAHE, so that their role would be limited to that of professional associations. These professional associations could conduct nationwide examinations to provide licenses for those wishing to enter the profession.

Financing

The expansion of our system of higher education, which is both necessary and desirable, is not possible without financing. For an increase in supply of quality education depends upon an increase in investment which, in turn, requires financial resources. There are several sources of such financing.

Government Support

There is no system of higher education in the world that is not based upon significant public outlays. And government financing will remain the cornerstone of any strategy to improve our system of higher education. The present support for higher education, at 0.7 per cent of GDP, is simply not adequate. In fact, over the past decade, in real terms, there has been a significant decline in the resources allocated for higher education, in the aggregate as also per student. In an ideal world, government support for higher education should be at least 1.5 per cent, if not 2 per cent of GDP, from a total of 6 per cent of GDP for education. This is easier said than done. But the government should endeavour to reach these levels by 2014. Even this magnitude of state financing, however, would not suffice for the massive expansion in higher education that is an imperative. Therefore, it is essential to explore a wide range of possibilities which can be complements to the increase in public expenditure.

Better Asset Management

Most public universities are sitting on a large reservoir of untapped resources in the form of land. In effect, with some imagination, many of our universities can be converted into institutions that are similar to land grant universities. Each university should thus have an innovative asset management plan. Such plans should be in consonance with objectives of universities. At the moment, however, universities have no strategy in this sphere. And there is considerable room to think in strategic terms about the use of physical assets in the possession of universities. It should be possible to draw up norms and parameters for universities to use their land as a source of finance.

Rationalization of Fees

On an average, fees constitute less than 10 per cent of total expenditure in our universities. And, in most universities, fees have remained unchanged for decades. In theory, universities have the freedom to decide on fees. In practice, however, universities have not exercised this freedom in part because of some genuine concerns about access but in larger part because of the rhetoric and populism in the political process. The problem has been compounded by the UGC method of providing grants-in-aid to bridge the difference between income and expenditure. Consequently, there is no incentive for universities or colleges to raise income through higher fees as that sum would be deducted from their UGC (or State government) grants. The low fees in public universities, without any means test, have meant unquantifiable benefits for unintended beneficiaries. But private players and foreign institutions have not been restrained in charging fees that the market can bear. The time has come to rethink, as we have no choice but to rationalise fees. It is for universities to decide the level of fees but, as a norm, fees should meet at least 20 per cent of the total expenditure in universities. In addition, fees need to be adjusted every two years through price indexation. Such small, continuous, adjustments would be absorbed and accepted far more easily than large, discrete changes after a period of time. This rationalisation of fees should be subject to two conditions: first, needy students should be provided with a fee waiver plus scholarships to meet their costs; second, universities should not be penalized by the UGC for the resources raised from higher fees through matching deductions from their grants-in-aid.

Philanthropic Contributions

It is clear that we have not exploited this potential. In fact, the proportion of such contributions in total expenditure on higher education has declined from more than 12 per cent in the 1950s to less than 3 per cent in the 1990s. It should be possible to nurture this tradition of philanthropy through changes in incentives for universities and for donors. In the present system, there is an explicit disincentive. If universities mobilize resources from elsewhere, they are in effect penalized through a matching deduction in their grant-in-aid What we need to do is exactly the opposite. Universities which mobilize resources through contributions should be rewarded with matching grants-in-aid. At present, there is also an implicit disincentive in both lax laws and trust laws. Endowments of universities can only be placed in specified securities where rates of return are low and barely keep up with rates of inflation. What is more, trusts must spend 85 per cent of the income stream from the endowment in the same year, so that only 15 per cent of the income stream can be used to build up the corpus in the endowment. These laws should be changed so that universities can invest in financial instruments of their choice and use the income from their endowments to build up a corpus.

Other Sources

Obviously, universities must not be driven by commercial considerations. But it would be both prudent and wise to tap other sources such as alumni contributions, licensing fees, or user charges (for facilities in universities used by people from outside). We need to create supportive institutional mechanisms that allow universities to engage professional firms for this purpose. Mobilizing resources, even from former students, is a task that cannot be performed by academics because it needs specialised talents and experience. Current UGC practice also penalises universities for any resources mobilised with a matching deduction from the grants-in-aid provided to the institution. Rather than penalizing universities for raising resources, the UGC should incentivise them. In addition, universities must have the autonomy and flexibility to mobilise resources from elsewhere by creating or using appropriate institutional mechanisms,

Private Investment

In three professions - engineering, medicine and management - there has been a *de facto* privatisation of education so that two-thirds to three-fourths of the seats are in private institutions. But private investment in university education, where more than 70 per cent of our students study, is almost negligible. It is essential to stimulate private investment in higher education as a means of extending educational opportunities. We must recognise that, even with the best will in the world, government financing cannot be enough to support the massive expansion in opportunities for higher education on a scale that is now essential.

Public-Private Partnerships

It might be possible to leverage public funding, especially in the form of land grants, to attract more (not-for-profit) private investment. The present system of allotment of land, where political patronage is implicit, discourages genuine educational entrepreneurs and encourages real estate developers in disguise. In principle, it should be possible to set up new institutions in higher education, not just more IITs and IIMs but also more universities, as public-private partnerships where the government provides the land and the private sector provides the finances. Such public-private partnerships which promote university-industry interface would also strengthen teaching and research.

International Students

India is not an attractive destination for international students, not even as much as it used to be 30 years ago. It is time for us to make a conscious attempt to attract foreign students to India for higher education. This would enrich our academic milieu. This would enhance quality. This would be a significant source of finance. Even 50,000 foreign students charged fees at an average rate of US$ 10,000 per annum would yield US$ 0.5 billion: the equivalent of Rs. 2300 crores per annum in current prices at current exchange rates. The other side of the coin is perhaps even more important. Estimates suggest that there are about 160,000 students from India studying abroad. If their average expenditure on fees and maintenance is US$ 25,000 per student per year, Indian students overseas are spending US$ 4 billion: the equivalent of Rs. 18,400 crores per annum in current prices at current exchange rates. This has an enormous potential as a source of finance for higher education in India, if only we could crate more opportunities for students with increased places and enhanced quality in our system.

Quality

The introduction of an independent regulator in higher education, the reform of existing public universities and the creation of national universities, taken together, would contribute to enhancement of quality in higher education. But this needs to be supported with some pro-active steps that would foster quality in higher education.

Accountability

The quality of higher education depends on a wide range of factors. But accountability, at every level, is a critical determinant. The higher education system must, therefore, provide for accountability *vis-a-vis* the outside world and create accountability within the system. Accountability of universities must not be confused with control of the state. Institutional mechanisms, based on checks and balances, constitute the most effective system for this purpose. The essential objective of accountability to society must be to empower students to take decisions rather than simply increase the power of the state. Stipulated performance criteria or inspections are forms of control. We need to create systems that enable students, or their parents, to choose between and assess universities.

Competition

The supply constraint on higher education is an impediment to accountability. When students have relatively few choices, institutions have greater power over them. An expansion of higher education which provides students with choices and creates competition between institutions is going to be vital in enhancing accountability. Such competition between institutions within India is, of course, essential. But the significance of competition from outside India, more qualitative than quantitative, must not be underestimated.

For this purpose, we must formulate appropriate policies for the entry of foreign institutions into India and the promotion of Indian institutions abroad. Such policies must ensure that there is an incentive for good institutions and a disincentive for sub-standard institutions to come to India. The present regime does the opposite: sub-standard players rush in while premier universities stay away as they care more about their autonomy and wish to set benchmarks for themselves. However, a level playing field should be ensured and all rules that apply to domestic institutions should also be applicable to foreign institutions. At the same time, policies must encourage rather than discourage Indian institutions to create campuses abroad not as business opportunities but as competition opportunities in their quest for academic excellence. Of course, expansion abroad should not be at the cost of domestic provision, either at present or in the future.

Accreditation

So far, we have sought to create accountability by increasing the powers of government regulators. Yet, it has done little to improve the quality of higher education. Consider, for example, the National Accreditation and Assessment Council (NAAC). This system has three characteristics which significantly erode its credibility. First, it grants one institution, the NAAC, monopoly power over accreditation. Second, NAAC itself does not have the capacity to rate all the institutions. It has rated just about 10 percent of the total number so far. Third, the methodology of NAAC is much too discretionary. Instead of vesting one institution created by the state with monopoly power, the IRAHE may be empowered to licence a number of accreditation agencies, public and private, to do the ratings. In doing so, the regulator would set standards for them. This will need to be accompanied by stringent information disclosure norms for all educational institutions, including the source and level of their accreditation. The rapid growth in higher education, particularly in the private sector, has created a strong need for empowering students and parents with reliable information from a credible accreditation process. This system can be supplemented with the creation of self-regulatory bodies in the higher education system and the freedom to seek recognition from global accreditation systems.

Internal Systems

In most universities, the main stakeholders, students, are minimally part of any mechanism for accountability. Obviously, student evaluations need to be used with care. Even so, they can be part of a baseline set of accountability measures which could at least establish whether classes scheduled in the timetable are held. But that is not all. Evaluation of courses and teachers by students is also needed, just as much as we need peer evaluation of teachers by teachers. Such internal systems of evaluation would strengthen accountability in the teaching-learning process. These must be combined with institutional mechanisms for accountability in other dimensions of university systems.

Information

Almost everywhere, information in the public domain is an important source of accountability. Higher education should be no exception. There should be disclosure norms for universities and institutions imparting higher education. They should be required to place basic information relating to their financial situation, physical assets, accreditation ratings, admissions criteria, faculty positions, academic curricula, and so on, in the public domain. This would empower students and parents and enable them to make informed choices. Information, along with competition, fostered by increased supply, will close the accountability loop.

Incentives

Even if we cannot introduce penalties for non-performance, it is necessary to introduce rewards for performance. We must, of course, recognise that universities are different from the hierarchical worlds in governments and corporate structures. The web of incentives is far more subtle. Even so, the time has come to think of salary differentials within and between Universities as a means of attracting and retaining talented faculty members. The salary differentiation among teachers within the same university needs to reflect the opportunity costs for teachers in some departments. This will help retain talent in some disciplines where remuneration in the market is much higher than in other subjects. Salary differentiation may enable some universities to develop centres of excellence in some disciplines. At the same time, it is important to ensure that disciplines which are essential for a good liberal education such as social sciences and humanities, as well as basic sciences which are not necessarily rewarded by the market, are given appropriate incentives to attract both teachers and students. Such salary differentials between -and within universities could be effective without being large. Indeed, there is a good reason to stipulate a maximum ratio for differences in salaries between faculty members so as not to threaten the identity of the professoriate. Obviously, universities cannot compete with salaries elsewhere, but they should endeavour to provide a comfortable minimum for all, with some premium for those who perform. It is also important to think of other incentives, such as housing, good facilities for teaching and research and some flexibility for non-teaching professional activities so long as these do not impinge on the primary responsibilities to the institution.

Differentiation

We have to recognize that there is bound to be diversity and pluralism in any system of higher education. Therefore, in a country as large as India, we cannot afford to adopt the principle that one-size-fits-all We must allow diversity to blossom. This could have many dimensions: curriculum, specialization, institutional architecture, students' composition, and so on. Similarly, differentiation is inevitable if not natural. Even if we do not wish to recognize it, such differentiation is a reality. Students and parents have clear preferences, possibly implicit rankings, based on their perceptions derived from available information. Our sense of pluralism must recognise, rather than ignore or shy away from, such diversity and differentiation. It is characteristic of every higher education system in the world. For higher education is about a quest for excellence. It is, at least in part, about distinction and not always about levelling. The institutions which excel are the important peaks that raise the average. They are also role models others seek to emulate. And institutions that become such role models could mentor and guide other selected institutions.

National Universities

We need to create substantial additional capacity in higher education for achieving a quantum jump in the gross enrolment ratio for a rapidly expanding population of young people. It would be expeditious to do so by simply expanding on our existing educational infrastructure. A fundamental paradigm shift in our understanding of quality and standards in higher education, however, requires creating completely new institutions that operate unconstrained by the current institutional and regulatory framework. We recommend the creation of up to 50 National Universities that can provide education of the highest standard. As exemplars for the rest of the nation, these universities shall train students in a variety of disciplines, including humanities, social sciences, basic sciences, commerce and professional subjects, at both the undergraduate and post-graduate levels. The number 50 is a long term objective. In the short run, it is important to begin with at least 10 such universities in the next 3 years. It is worth noting that the National Universities need not all be new universities. Some of the existing universities could also be converted into National Universities, on the basis of rigorous selection criteria, to act as exemplars. We recognise that there could be a human resource constraint if faculty members are not available in adequate numbers to establish these universities. But, for such centres of academic excellence, it should be possible to attract talent from among those who choose other professions in India or the academic profession outside India.

National Universities can be established in two ways, by the government, or by a private sponsoring body that sets up a Society, Charitable Trust or Company. Since public finance is an integral constituent of universities worldwide, most of the new universities shall need significant initial financial support from the government. This could be in several forms. Each university may be endowed with a substantial *allocation of public land,* in excess of its spatial requirements. The excess land can be a subsequent source of income generation, its value rising over time due to the growing stature of the university. In the case of privately executed Charitable Trusts, exceptions need to be made in existing Income Tax laws to encourage large *endowments.* In particular, there should be no restriction on the utilization of income in any given time period, the Trusts should be allowed to invest their funds in financial instruments of their choice, and all proceeds from the sale of capital assets should be exempt from capital gains tax. These universities shall have the autonomy to invest in financial instruments of their choice, by employing private fund managers if required. Appropriate mechanisms also need to be put in place for the optimal *management of physical assets,* like laboratories, libraries, classrooms and other facilities. Finally, these universities shall have the autonomy to set *student fee levels* and tap other spurges for generating funds such as industry collaborations, overseas operations, as also commercial use of university facilities and alumni networks.

The National Universities we propose shall admit students on an all-India basis. They shall adopt the principle of *needs-blind admissions,* thereby ensuring that an applicant's ability or inability to pay shall not influence the admission decision made by a university. Further, once admitted, the university should ensure that no student has to forego his/her place due to financial constraints. This will require a host of scholarships, freeships, bursaries and awards for economically disadvantaged students. At the undergraduate level, a nationwide test that objectively measures the verbal, quantitative and analytical abilities of applicants shall be administered by an independent testing body. Admissions shall be based on a combination of Class XII results, scores from the nationwide test, application materials including written work and personal statements, as also interviews. At the postgraduate level, admissions shall be based on a combination of the applicant's academic record, application materials, interviews and academic or professional references that indicate his/her aptitude for further studies in the relevant discipline.

Undergraduate degrees in the National Universities shall have a duration of three years so that these are in conformity with the duration of undergraduate courses elsewhere in India. In the first year, students shall have the opportunity to study foundation, analytical and tools courses before choosing a specific discipline in the second year. They shall also have the option, at the end of the second year, of completing an integrated five-year master's degree. Degrees should be granted on the basis of completing a requisite number of credits, obtained from different courses. Each student shall be required to earn a minimum number of credits in his/her chosen discipline, and shall have the freedom to earn the rest from courses in other disciplines. The academic year shall therefore be semester-based and students shall be internally evaluated at the end of each course. Transfer of credits from one National University to another shall also be possible. A wide variety of courses shall be offered, in traditional academic disciplines, employment-oriented specific areas and cross-cutting competencies. Syllabi shall be revised every year to keep up with changes and current developments in various disciplines. Departments that do not update their syllabus for two consecutive years shall be asked to provide justification. Students shall have the option of taking up internships in private companies or research institutions in lieu of a certain number of credits.

An appropriate system of appointments and incentives is required to maximize the productivity of faculty in the National Universities. There shall be scope for salary differentials between National Universities and also between disciplines. Faculty training will be contingent on periodical reviews of research *output* and student evaluation. The most accomplished faculty members shall be encouraged to teach undergraduate courses. There shall be no career advancement schemes and appointments at every level shall be through open competition. The total number of faculty positions may be specified, but there should be complete flexibility in choosing the level at which faculty appointments are made, so that, for talented faculty members, career paths are not constrained by the number of vacancies. In order to maintain the quality of the National Universities, mechanisms should be in place to monitor and evaluate the performance and progress of teachers including peer reviews. The procedures and results of these evaluations will be open and transparent.

The research outputs of these universities shall be vital contributors to India's socio-economic development and progress in science and technology. Strong linkages shall be forged between teaching and research, universities and industry, and universities and research laboratories.

The National Universities shall be department-based and shall not have any affiliated colleges. Each department will administer undergraduate and post-graduate courses. Non-teaching functions should be outsourced wherever possible, and a maximum ratio of 2:1 should be maintained between non-teaching and teaching staff. Each university should appoint an internal ombudsman for the redressal of faculty, staff, student and public grievances. Administrative processes, wherever possible, should be streamlined and made transparent and accountable by the use of information and communications technology.

Access

Education is an essential mechanism for inclusion through the creation of social opportunities. It is, therefore, essential that in addition to ensuring that no student is denied the opportunity to participate in higher education due to financial constraints, access to education for economically and historically socially underprivileged students is enhanced in a substantially more effective manner.

Economic barriers to higher education can be addressed by ensuring financial viability for all students wanting to enter the world of higher education. This can be done through two strategies. One is to adopt a *needs blind admissions* policy. This would make it unlawful for educational institutions to take into account any financial factor while deciding whether or not to admit a student. Every institution will be free to use a variety of instruments to achieve this aim: scholarships or cross-subsidies. In addition, academic institutions would be able to set a fee of their own choice subject to the provision that there are at least two banks that are willing to finance the entire cost of education at that institution, without any collateral other than the fact of admission. The cost of education includes not just fees but also reasonable living expenses including costs such as hostel and mess fees and any other expenses associated with the course of study. Since commercial banks may be wary of funding economically deprived students, especially in non-professional courses, we need a well-funded and extensive National Scholarship Scheme targeting economically underprivileged students and students from historically socially disadvantaged groups, particularly students from rural and backward areas. The success of this proposal depends on generous government support. For instance, the government should endeavour to make available about 100,000 scholarships for such students. These scholarships should be set at a level where students are empowered to go to any institution of their choice.

We also need to undertake more proactive forms of affirmative action to ensure inclusion of marginal and excluded groups. Reservations are essential but they are a part, and one form of, affirmative action. Disparities in educational attainments are related to caste and social groups, but are also strongly related to other indicators such as income, gender, region and place of residence. Access to quality higher education is further limited for students from certain types of schools. Therefore deprivation of educational opportunities is a multi-dimensional problem and attention needs to be paid to different salient levels of deprivation faced by students. A meaningful and comprehensive framework would account for the multi-dimensionality of differences that still persist. Such a deprivation index could provide weighted scores to students and the cumulative score could be used to supplement a student's school examination score. After adding the score from the deprivation index, all students could compete for admissions.

The indicators need to be easily identifiable and verifiable for the system to work effectively. They should cover the different types of disadvantages that a student could face at the school level, and while applying for admissions to higher education. This system serves the dual purpose of considering various disadvantages and ensuring that a reserved category student who has otherwise enjoyed other benefits does not get great preference at the time of admissions.

Illustrative indicators of backwardness that need to be measured by such an index could include *social background* covering caste (keeping in view regional variations), religion and gender, *family education history; fantffy income, type of school* distinguishing between government and private schools and between schools from different locations, the medium of instruction, *place of residence* distinguishing between urban and rural areas and accounting for regional deprivation by sotting districts along an index of infrastructure or access to social benefits and *physical disability.*

Globalisation in Education

Some Negative Implications in Higher and Technical Education of India

*—Dr. H.C. Das**

*—Dr. S.N. Das***

Introduction

Education, Health and Housing are major components of social infrastructure of an economy. Without these basic activities and services, the efficiency and productivity of the work force cannot increase and in consequence economic growth of the country cannot be accelerated. Education & training make fuller and rational utilization of surplus man-power by providing larger and better job opportunities in both rural and urban areas of the country. This, in turn, raises income and living standards of the people. A rational educational system produces required skill needed by the economy and society. Hence, it is a pre-condition of technological change.

During British period, education had not made in progress. In 1951, barely 16.7 per cent of the population was literate. After Independence only great progress has been achieved in the field of education. After opening up of Indian Economy with the principle of globalisation since 1991, the educational processes of the country has changed greatly. Both literacy rates and quality education have improved a lot. In 2011, literacy rate of the country has been 74.04 per cent. Since the 1990's 'globalisation' is the new buzzword. Globalisation

*Lecturer in Economics, Ganjam College, Ganjam.

**Reader in Commerce, Ganjam College, Ganjam.

principle opens the economy to foreign investment and more competition. The new policy of globalisation in India which got a boost by late Prime Minister Rajiv Gandhi and P.V. Narasimha Rao aims at making the Indian economy competitive in all respects and much better integrated with the world economy. In fact, globalisation is the expansion of markets for goods, services, capital and labour beyond national boundaries. The main characteristics of a globalised economy are that State intervention is replaced to a large extent by market forces, nationalisation yields place to privatisation and restrictions are replaced by freedom of choice and actions. In fact, with adoption of globalisation and liberalisation of policy since 1990's, our economy is developing fast. Industries and corporates are going globalised, tremendous changes are being felt in I.T., manufacturing and service sector like education. More and more sectors opened up for foreign direct investments in various sectors namely Telecommunication, roads, ports, airports, insurance etc. Thus, the process of globalisation not only includes opening up of world trade and internationalisation of financial markets, it also includes development of means of communication, migration of population, more mobility of labour, data and ideas between different countries. The impact of globalisation is visible everywhere including education.

Under these circumstances, there is much need of development of human capital through proper system of education. More and more educated man power are to be created in the country which can meet the growing demands of the various sectors due to massive doses of foreign investment in various sectors taking place at present and much of investment to take place in future due to the impact of globalisation.

Objectives of the Study

The present study is undertaken with the following objectives:

1. To study how far globalisation in Education in India has resulted in improvement in productivity of human beings.

2. Whether the present education system has benefited persons of all income brackets and the entire community.
3. Whether the globalisation in education has succeeded in bringing quality education in the country.
4. To disclose some of the negative implications of present system of globalisation in education.

Growth of Higher and Technical Education System in the Country

A country's socio-economic development is directly proportional to its education systems. In order to take over nation to dizzy heights in this period of globalisation, we need to spread education to its every corner. At the same time, the higher education should be modern in content and methodology along with technical education.

In the constitutional amendment of 1976, education was included in the concurrent list. Since then the Central govt. continued to play a leading role in the evolution and monitoring of educational policies and programmes. Accordingly the national policy of education (NPE), 1986 was declared. After globalisation? the programme of action, 1986 was updated in 1992. The modified National educational policy among other things envisaged a National system of education to bring about a uniformity in education, providing universal access, retention and quality in education and expanding a structure of higher education.

Higher Education

India's Higher Education System is the third largest in the World, after China and U.S.A. The main governing body is the University Grants commission (UGC) which enforces its standards, advises the Government and helps coordinate between the centre and state. The UGC was established in November 1956 as a statutory body of Government of India through an act of Parliament, has been vested with two main responsibilities, that of coordination, determination and maintenance of standards in higher education and that of providing funds to achieve its objects. The growth of higher education has been phenomenal since India's independence at which time there were 20 Universities and 500 Colleges. The total profile of the type and number of higher education institutes is summarized in Table No. 3.1.

TABLE 3.1: List of University Level Educational Institutions

(As on 31.12.2010)

Sl. No.	*Institutional Category*	*No. of Institutions*
1.	Central Universities	42
2.	Institutions Deemed to be Universities	130
3.	State Universities	261
4.	Private Universities	73
5.	Institutions of National importance	33
6.	Institutions established under State Legislatures Acts	5
	Total number of Institutions	544
7.	No. of Colleges	
	(a) Recognized U/s.2 (f) of the UGC Act, 1956	7,450
	(b) Recognized U/s. 12(B) of the UGC Act, 1956	6,028

Of the 42 Central Universities, 38 were given maintenance and development grant by the UGC. The IGNOU, New Delhi, the Central Agricultural University (CAU), Imphal and the Indian Maritime University (IMU) Chennai are being funded by the Union Ministry of Human Resource Development, the Ministry of Agriculture and the Ministry of Shipping and Transport respectively. Of the 334 State Universities, the UGC has been making budgetary plan allocation for only 133, excluding medical and agricultural Universities.

Important policy initiatives taken by the Government with regard to higher education are—National Commission for

Higher Education, National Accreditation Regulatory Authority, Prohibition of unfair practices in Technical Educational Institutions, Medical Educational institutions and University Bill, 2010, Educational tribunals, the Foreign Educational Institutions (Regulation of entry and operations) Bill, Academic Reforms, Inclusive Education, quality improvement etc.

Technical Education

In 2010-2011 there were 79 Centrally-funded institutions in the country, the 79 Centrally-funded institutions of Technical and Science Education are as follows (Table 3.2):

TABLE 3.2 : Number of Centrally-funded Technical Institutions

Sl. No.	*Type of Institutions*	*Numbers*	
		Existing at the end of the Xth plan	*Established during XIth plan*
1.	IITs	7	8
2.	NITs	20	10
3.	IIITs	4	20
4.	IISERs	2	3
5.	IIMs	6	7
6.	SPAs	1	2

As the table reveals the Education System in India consists of three major components - general education, vocational & technical education. Till globalisation of the economy, these were State responsibility. Since liberalisation and globalisation of the economy the education sector has been opened up for private sector and for the joint venture of investment. Both higher education and technical education play a vital role in human resource development of the country by creating skilled man power, enhancing industrial productivity and improving the quality of life. India's higher education system is the third largest in the world after China and USA. Technical education covers course and programmes in engineering, technology, management, architecture, town planning, pharmacy and applied arts and crafts, hotel management and catering technology. The technical educational system at present in the country can be broadly classified into three categories-Central Government Funded Institutions, State Government/ State Funded Institutions and Self financed institutions.

The Government of India brought the private universities establishment and regulation bill in 1995 after globalisation started to encourage the setting up of private universities. The Ministry of HRD also set-up a core group of 6 members drawn from private sector, reputed institutions and experts to obtain their views and recommendations on private sector participation in higher education. The group observed that there was an urgent need to enable private sector to be operative in the field of education in a big way. The rules and regulations should be such that the foreign students are also attracted to study in India. Another characteristic feature of globalisation in education system is private universities are to bring about excellence in education and make the students on par with their foreign counterparts in knowledge skill and information's—like the students of Universities of Harvard, Yale, Cambridge, Oxford. More of self-financing courses offered by the Universities considering their demand and market response.

Some Negative Implications of Globalisation in Education

Globalisation in the system of Education of the country has far reaching effect. At the same time, the present system of education-both higher and technical-face major challenges which have also dangerous consequences. We have enumerated below some of the negative implications of globalisation of education, particularly when education sector is opened up for the private sectors:

1. Enormous growth of private educational institutions which have become quite commercial, a commodity sold in the market only to the highest bidder.
2. Enormous growth of coaching institutions and rising trend of private tuitions.
3. An impression is given to the students that their aim in life is to pass the university examination and fetch a lucrative job with high salary.
4. A majority of young persons with poor economic back grounds go for general education and after the completion of education they have to struggle hard to fulfill their basic requirements which obviously brings in them a deep sense of frustration and confusion.
5. Educational system at the secondary as well as at the University level is not in accordance with preparing ground for changing socio-economic scenario after globalisation. There is lack of uniformity in examination and evaluation system between different states, the syllabus is unwieldly and redundant.
6. The system of education at present teaches young educated mass who receive vocational and technical education from reputed institutions to sell their intelligence or intellectual resources to business and corporate houses for the benefits of business community in lieu of a hand some amount of money.
7. The educated youth are directed to carry out efficiently the business plan and programmes of corporates and implement them with sincerity, or else the chance of loosing job is very high.
8. Limited resources are allocated to state-led educational institutions, hence staffing pattern is inadequate. The parents are interested to send their wards to the private institutions, as a result of which quality education is not being imparted in govt. led institutions. Moreover, accountability is not laid down

on teachers, in case of poor performance in govt.-owned institutions.

9. Another important negative implications of present system of education is that the highest payer is assured a place in educational institutions of high repute and no attention is paid to merit. In order words, during post globalisation there has been total commercialisation of education and charging of capitation fee is an open manifestation.
10. No provision or no importance is given to inculcate human values in the present system of education in the students, though its importance has been aptly emphasised by educationists and education commission.
11. The curricula are not properly formulated to bring about a conscious internalization of healthy work ethics and values of a humane and composite culture. Hence deterioration of human values in the society is noticed. The values which are universally acceptable such as non-violence, righteousness, truthfulness, honesty, discipline, helpfulness, sympathy, charity, peace, fraternity etc. are disappearing in thfeodays of globalisation.
12. The UGC recently has introduced a scheme of value education at the Universities and College levels to promote value education among students and teachers, i.e. to be sympathetic not only to human beings but also to the animal kingdoms, the forestry and the environment but its implications and applications have remained far from satisfactory.
13. The private players in the system of education are encashing the students hunger for higher education and establishing private colleges in every Indian state, so also private Universities, as the present state run Universities are in capable of providing enough seats for the willing and serious students who intend to pursue higher studies.

14. The private universities invite the students and paint the rosy pictures of higher education but without any guarantee of job after completion of the degree and diploma. The guarantee is only for a certificate, at a price.
15. Globalisation in education has resulted in growth of private Universities which are more like business houses then educational centers. They run on the fee of the students. The expenditure of the running the University is quite high-including high cost of building infrastructure, salaries of highly qualified teaches and other staffs and day to day expenses and payment of electricity, telephone, water bills and taxes. As a result fee structure of the students is increased.
16. The atmosphere institutions of education during these days is full of competitions. The students are thought to excel one another and enjoy the material comfort. Their competitions become so intense that it leads to rivalries, jealousy and hatred among class fellows.

In short, the major challenges before the higher and technical education system is one of access, equity and inclusion. Another area of concern is the inadequate availability of faculty both in terms of quality and in numbers. Promotion of R & D efforts, improvement in employability of trained graduates and post graduates coming out of the technical institutes where efforts are required if globalisation in education is to put long lasting effect in the economy.

Conclusion

Human Development is an important parameter for the well being of the society. The important factors which creates conducive environment for human development are freedom, equity, justice, literacy, fairness, health care etc. The most critical ones are to lead a long and healthy life, to be educated and to enjoy a decent standard of living. A well nourished, healthy, educated, skilled labour is the most important productive asset. Thus investments in nutrition, health services and education are justified on ground of productivity.

However, India ranked 134 out of 187 countries in terms of Human Development Index in 2011, though India's HDI value increased from 0.344 to 0.547 for 2011 over 1980. India's HDI value is below the countries of medium human development group and below the countries in South Asia. The HDI of India is much lower than that of China and Sri Lanka, but only a shade better than those of Pakistan, Bangladesh and Nepal.

To conclude it may be said that the growing education facilities that are made available and expected to be made available in India during these days of globalisation would no doubt better take care of the growing young population in the country and make them skilled enough, but the problem lies in the fact that how many of our young population would be able to avail such facilities which are very costly affair. The doubt persists in how far modern system of higher and technical education would be at the reach of the common masses, the marginalized groups, the SCs, STs, OBCs, Minorities, Physically challenged, the weaker and poorer sections of the society who are deprived of basic necessities of life. Therefore, policy makers must pay serious attention to it and try to address the concerns with concerted efforts and judicious planning, so that, globalisation in higher and technical education of the country becomes more inclusive and more effective so as to exert positive impact on the economy.

REFERENCES

M.B.Sukla: Indian Economy, Taxmann Publications, 2012.

National Institute of Technology Act, 2007

The Central Educational Institutions, (Reservations in Administration) Act, 2006,

UGC reports, 11th FYP (2007-12)

Strengthening of Higher Education
Measures to be Adopted

*—Dr. D. Tata Rao**

Introduction

The permeable of our Constitution proclaims equality of status and opportunity to all its citizens. Even the Supreme Court holds that human dignity, equality of status and opportunity are integral to the right to life, and the education is a cardinal component of human dignity. Hence, it is needless to stress that the state and central government are under constitutional obligation to provide a fair level of education to all its citizens irrespective of the social, financial, regional and religious considerations.

Equitable development of any nation in the emerging knowledge economy is linked up with massive acquisition and distribution, which turns out to be the most important capital input in production. Universalisation of excellence in higher education is a necessary pre-condition for success in the competitive global scenario. Under the impact of Grobalisation, liberalisation, privatisation (LPG) the educational system is slowly getting commercialised. Neither the State nor the central government ever thought of creating a suitable machinery to contain commercialisation of education system. Further, the state governments one after the other are

*Lecturer in Commerce, S.G.A. Government Degree College, Yellamanchili, Visakhapatnam Distt. Andhra Pradesh.

denigrating the public sector including education. Management of education is steadily getting into the hands of the affluent section of our social sest up. In this process, the poor would ultimately deprive of their legitimate right to higher education at a low set, which they hither to have been made use of. Deprivation may drive the poor into despair. Democracy then becomes barbaric. The root cause for such a situation, ultimately stand out to be the abrogation of a constitutional right that guarantees equal opportunity and social justice.

Apart from the above, it is known fact that intelligence, aptitude and talent do not coincide normally with the economic and social status of the individuals. Therefore, there is a need to keep the higher education accessible to the poor and the needy at a low cost, failing which a large number of the people with talent and potential for significant contribution to national development may have to be denied access to higher education on the grounds of individual's financial inability to meet the cost. Therefore, it is desirable in the national interest to strengthen the public funded educational institutions and to enable them to withstand the private and foreign institutions in the global market in terms of quality and cost.

The national interest to strengthen the public funded educational institutions and to enable them to withstand the private and foreign institutions in the global market in terms of quality and cost.

In this context, Government of Andhra Pradesh and the College teachers working in public funded institutions (Government Colleges and Aided Colleges) should initiate certain ameliorative measures in order to enable these institutions to be competitive in global market and thereby meet the equity concerns of our social set-up.

Autonomy and Accountability

Autonomy implies freedom for an organization or an individual to govern itself or himself independently. But the autonomous functioning depends upon the one's ability or the capabilities of an organization to act and make decisions without being controlled.

That being what autonomy implies, Kothari Commission (1966) conceived autonomy as a sub-system within the larger affiliating system. Therefore, autonomous colleges were allowed to enjoy a greater degree of academic freedom in comparison with those of non-autonomous colleges m the system. The objective was to give a comfortable position with reference to academic innovations in admission, designing of courses and conduct of examinations. The parent university's role was confined to general supervision and actual conferment of degrees. But there was no agenda for dismantling the affiliating system. This concept of autonomy underwent a radical change in National Policy on Education, (NPE 1986) that projected affiliating system as the root of all evils in higher education and autonomy was used as a weapon to dismantle the affiliating system. The University Grants Commission (UGG) on Xth Plan profile of Higher Education went a step further, and resorted to selective differential funding to promote the implementation of the new policy on autonomy. An institution identified as autonomous was allowed financial support worth Rs. 1.72 crores. An institution that was not autonomous but accredited by the NAAC got Rs. 70 Lakhs. An institution that has potential for academic excellence but neither has autonomous status nor accredited by NAAC got only Rs. 35 lakhs. Despite such efforts, there has been little enthusiasm in the establishment of autonomous colleges. So far there are only 197 autonomous colleges in the country. In Andhra Pradesh there are only 18 autonomous colleges.

NIEPA (National Institute of Educational Planning and Administration) study on autonomous colleges (1987) came out with the observations that while teachers were involved in decision-making process on Academic matters, Administrative and Financial matters were confined to bureaucratic control. The attempts to refashion or redesign of course contents were strongly influenced by the ongoing pattern of courses in the country. But for some changes here and there, diversification of courses and course combinations were mainly conformed to traditional forms. Thus the efforts towards academic excellence had fallen short of desired levels.

Despite such large-scale criticism about the actual performance of autonomous colleges, there was no let up in the official patronage of autonomous colleges. The ideology of LPG has become the guiding principle of governance since early nineties. It has given further fillip to official patronage of autonomy in all its forms. The report of the CABE (Central Advisory Board on Education) Committee, 2005 on autonomy has filled up the policy gaps and systematically sidelined the concept of academic autonomy mooted by Kothari Commission and has put financial autonomy at the center stage.

Autonomy is freedom allowed for facilitating administrative and academic decisions in the educational institutions. But autonomy and accountability go hand in had. One cannot be without the other. Accountability implies transparency with answerability that enables decision-making. In other terms, accountability is the responsibility vested with an organization or the individuals to attain a set goal. Further, accountability is related to 'return'. In this context, a teachers should ensure that student learns what he or she has been taught. UGC classified teacher duties as: (*i*) Teaching (*ii*) Research (*iii*) Extension and Management. The UGC stipulates for a teacher 40 hours of working in a week to cover the above activities. It is to be noted that if the teaching hours for an undergraduate class is 16 hours, it means sufficient time should be spared for the preparation of classroom 'Lecture'. The preparation hours for the post-graduate class is more than the teaching hours. Thus, lower teaching hours and higher preparatory hours are indicating an inverse relation between teaching and preparatory hours. Many teachers do not realize the fact that preparatory hours for teaching are important inputs for quality education.

Teachers who do not devote their time for preparation are adding to the loss of quality in education. The accountability of a teacher to devote his time for preparation should not remain unnoticed. There is also an inverse relationship between teaching and research. At the post-graduate level, normally teacher has less of teaching hours and more of research hours. If the research goes unnoticed in the calculation of accountability then also, the quality of education suffers. There are some other responsibilities that a teacher has to perform. In this context, autonomy has to be defined and understood as 'freedom with social responsibility'.

In view of the above position, it is desirable and appropriate that the State Government initiate steps to accord total autonomy to all the public funded Government or Aided Colleges and allow the teachers to play a vital role in decision making pertaining to academic, administrative and financial matters without keeping them under the remote control and the teachers in turn hold themselves' accountable for the performance of the institution. Autonomy and accountability should go together in order to enable the public funded institutions of higher learning to face the global competition.

Collective Excellence

There is a need to build 'synergy'. One's expertise in one's own area, when clubbed with two or three, it is possible to develop 'collective excellence' in many areas and share the resources through a network in the common interest to achieve the goals of higher education.

We would be able to generate a mechanism through which sharing and optimum utilisation of resources among the 'cluster colleges' can be visualised as a possibility. It is unfortunate that we teachers working in colleges are segregating ourselves from other levels of education-primary, secondary and higher secondary. The colleges should own up the responsibility of updating the knowledge of the teachers working in the feeder institutions instead of blaming them for the substandard teaching. Many teachers in schools are not provided with adequate opportunity to update their knowledge in the relevant subjects. Colleges can collectively organise in-service training and help them to be more effective in handling their job responsibilities. The potential strength and resources of the teachers in colleges, are in fact, under-utilised. We are living in an age of inclusion but not exclusion. It is quite possible for us to make our colleges establish 'collective excellence' and meet the requirements of schools in the vicinity instead of distancing ourselves and remain in isolation. The college and school teacher organisations can play a vital rote in developing 'collective excellence' and put our resources to the optimum utilisation.

In fact for any reform or change, those who respond fall under five categories:

(*i*) Innovators,
(*ii*) The early adopters,
(*iii*) The adopters,
(*iv*) Late adopters and
(*v*) Laggards.

The second and the fifth category generally constitute 10% of the total number of we throw the idea of 'Collective Excellence' at 180 Government Colleges, atleast 18 colleges in the state may come forward to form into a cluster and this will have its impact on the rest. Innovator innovates new ideas whether we like it or not. There is joy in working together and working better than growing in isolation.

Constitution of Educational Service

There should be a clear-cut policy with reference to recruitment of College Teachers. At present, Government of Andhra Pradesh is running all the public funded educational institutions without recruiting the teachers on permanent basis in accordance with the rules in force. The government introduced the concept of part-time lecturers with full time workload and posted them against the vacant post of lecturers to turn out the workload attached to the post while denying them the scale of pay attached to the post. They are paid a paltry amount of Rs. 5,000 a month, when they stand entitled to the scale of pay of Rs. 8,000-13,500. Of course, some of the part-time lectures are appointed again as lecturer on permanent basis while rendering them ineligible for pensionary benefits. The private managements, taking into consideration the concept of 'part-time lecturer' developed by the Government-Model Employer, further exploited them by reducing their pay from Rs. 5,000 to Rs. 2,000 a month. In our social set up, even the uneducated and unskilled workers are well protected with reference to their wages under the minimum wages Act, but not the well qualified personnel who are wedded to the teaching profession. As on this day. nowhere in the world a teacher is subjected to such a humiliating situation.

Government of Andhra Pradesh accepted the principle that all the college and university teachers working in the State should be brought on to UGC pay structure and revise the same as an when this pay structure is subjected to revision.

It is unfortunate to note that the principle accepted nearly three decades ago is no sought to be distorted while implementing UGC scales of pay to the college and university teachers. There are several instances of deviations in the recent times with reference to adoption of the pay scales, conversion of D.A. (Dearness Allowance) into D.P. (Dearness Pay), pensionary benefits, sanction of incentive increments etc. that hurt the fine sentiments of the teachers. They feel hurt no on account of getting less emoluments but these deviations from the accepted principle reflects prejudicial attitude of the government towards teachers. It is appropriate' and correct on the part of the government to adhere to a principle consistently while deciding on these matters.

Government of Andhra Pradesh in due regard for the recommendations of the Kothari Commission (1964-66) in its chapter 'Educational Administration and Supervision' decided to bring out a comprehensive Education Act, covering various aspects of the problems pertaining to educational system in the state. A committee was constituted in the year 1974 under the Chairmanship of Sri M.V. Rajagopal, I.A.S., to draft the bill. This Bill was passed into an Act (Act 1 of 1982) and the Government of Andhra Pradesh instead of taking action in accordance with the provisions contained in this Act, issued several executive instructions from time to time that are contrary to the provisions of the Act. According to section 78 of the Act, the Government is expected to constitute 'Educational Service' in order to regulate recruitment of school and college teachers. Further, the Government appear to have been reluctant to constitute 'Educational Service' for the reasons best known to themselves. Ignoring the sections 73 and 74 of the Act, Government have absorbed a good number of college teachers from taken over colleges and clubbed them with the others who had already been organized into local cadres. The authorities concerned do not realize the fact that all the executive instructions ought to be in agreement with the statutes but not in contravention to them. The posts of principal are of vital importance in Higher Education, These posts should be filled as per the rules in force, Government of Andhra Pradesh have been filling up these posts since 1994 ignoring the statutes that prescribed qualifications to hold the posts and procedures to select the suitable candidates.

As on this day there are 160 vacant posts of principals in Government Colleges. They have not been filled on the pretext that a case pertaining to seniority of the Lecturers is pending in Supreme Court. Infact, that case has nothing to do with the filling up of the vacant pots. It is unfortunate that the Government of Andhra Pradesh is equating ageing with seniority, ignoring the fact that seniority implies-expertise in the field. It is true that there are several cases pertaining to service conditions of teachers that are pending in various judicial forums. But the Government and administrative authorities at the helm of affairs should analyze and find out the reasons for these prolonged litigations. Government should make its stand clear and frame rules to be observed with reference to service conditions of the teachers. Government or any subordinate authority should restrain themselves from issuing any executive instruction in contravention to statutes. If the Government were to think and decide that the statutory orders go against the public interest, the same can be amended to meet the public interest but it is highly undesirable to violate the rule of law.

A careful study of prolonged litigations in judicial forums especially pertaining to the education department reveals the fact that they are all cropped up as a result of executive instructions that run contrary to certain statutory orders. Hence, there is a need for enactment of statutory regulations that deal with service matters of the teachers. The rules and regulations should be unambiguous in their expression and meaning without giving scope for different interpretations. This is how we can reduce the litigations in the department to its minimum.

In the circumstances stated above the Government should give up *ad hoc* and stop-gap arrangements with reference to recruitment of college teachers including principals of Government Colleges and constitute 'Educational Service' as envisaged through AP education Act, 1982. Government should fill up at least 80% of the posts in Government and aided colleges on permanent basis. The part time lecturers/ guest faculty can take care of the remaining workload. Keeping in view the quantum of work-load, the part time Lecturers should be allowed the minimum of the scale of pay attached to the post. If need be, there must be a minimum wages act to regulate and ensure respectable payment to the teachers wherever they work.

Time Bound Settlement of Grievances

Human beings normally act and operate with emotions and instincts. Human responses depend upon how his basic needs are met. When he is satisfied, he may go into a secure environment, wherein he begins to think of himself and his inner urge for creative activity. If he is driven to suffer from the sense of gross injustice, the inner urge in him for creating something better, shall not be invoked into activity in any human. One has to understand the simple phenomena in our educational system that a teacher with stress, strain and tension is a liability and the one who has been free of all these is an asset to the institution.

Teachers are very sensitive and they normally feel highly frustrated if they are not allowed their due pertaining to their service conditions. Infact they are petty issues like; withholding of pay fixations, annual grade increments, delay in promotions etc. There is no reason as to why administration should delay in responding to their requests. There is an exemplary case that marks at the efficacy of the Administration. A principal applied for his pensionary benefits in the year 1979. He passed away in the year 2005. His legal heirs are still pursuing pension papers in the office of the Director of Collegiate Education. Long wait killed the petitioner but not the pendency.

Government orders pertaining to service conditions of the teachers are not implemented immediately. Nearly two years ago, government issued orders instructing the Director of Collegiate Education to count the service rendered as Junior Lecturer for the purpose of Career Advancement Scheme. These orders haven't yet been implemented. Further, the office of the Directorate of Collegiate Education very often resorts to different interpretations of the Government orders at different periods of time. The same orders can be interpreted to benefit a person now, and deny the benefit at a later date with a different interpretation. This type of misinterpretation of Government orders should be viewed seriously. One should realize the fact than a man of conscience shall not bear it any more.

Kothari Commission (1964-66) strongly opines that the Administration in educational system should serve teaching and research, but in practice it happens rarely. It would be of immense value and great service to the teachers if the Government were to create a suitable machinery to redress the individual grievances of the teachers.

The office of the Directorate of Collegiate Education should ensure time bound settlement of the cases that have been kept pending for more than six months.

Financing Higher Education

Education is a public good since the benefits accrue to all as opposed to the private good, which is consumed by an individual. Higher Education is also a social investment and is a merit good. So far, the share of public expenditure on education in terms of GDP has never touched a figure of 6% as stipulated by the Kothari Commission. Global Scenario demands higher share of public financing for higher education. The gross enrolment ratio of relevant age group in higher education is only 7 per cent and that needs to be raised to a level of 20 per cent by 2020 in this context, recommendations of Justice Punftaiah Committee should be taken into consideration. A reasonable amount 15 per cent to 25 per cent of the annual recurring expenditure should be collected from the students as a tuition fee.

Recently, APSCHE (Andhra Pradesh State Council of Higher Education) has suggested certain reforms in the field of higher education with reference to duration of the degree course, combinations and introduction of ICT and a course in communicative skills at under-graduate and post-graduate level. These reforms are suggested keeping in view the global trend in the field. Hence, it is appropriate that the teachers working in Government and Aided Colleges should take initiative and see that they are implemented in Public Funded Institutions on priority basis. Otherwise, these institutions may lag behind when compared to their counterparts under the management of the corporate sector. Under the market economy, one has to watch the global trends in the field of education and keep oneself abreast of the latest.

These are some of the measures that required to be adopted with immediate effect in order to strengthen the Public Funded Educational Institutions of higher learning in view of our equity concerns.

Quality Circles in Higher Education
Empirical Evidences

*–Dr. R.N. Misra**
*–G. Chandrayya***

Introduction

There is no dispute on the issue of the need to ensure quality in education. This need for quality manifests itself in the inability of the education system to provide good moral values. At the most vital point it manifests itself in a feeling of dejection and low satisfaction among the teaching faculty, disillusionment among students, and a detached attitude among demonstrators. It is therefore imperative that deliberate and conscious efforts be made to ensure quality in the system. In our competitive environment, quality management has gained wide importance in industrial circles and is gradually being introduced and experimented with in higher education.

Quality control system must cover the systems and processes that underpin institutions' responsibilities for teaching and learning. It should also encompass output standards aimed at and achieved by students. The quality of education can be enhanced when administrators, teachers, staff and education board members develop new attitudes that focus on leadership, team work, cooperation, accountability and recognition. It has been aptly said that

*Prof. of M.B.A. in SMIT, Berahmpur, Orissa.

**Reading Commerce (A.P.)

money is not the key to improve the quality of education. The hub of all development is the human factor.

The Concept

Quality circles have played a dynamic role in improving quality and productivity in every sector. Their contribution in Japan is particularly hailed and emulated world over. Quality circles, a highly culture in:

- Ms. Shobha Rani is Guest Faculty at the Department of Post Graduate Studies in Commerce, University of Mysore and Ms. Madhu Priya is a Masters Student at the Post Graduate Centre, Hassan.

Tegrated movement, evolved in Japan in the early 60s. The first quality circle, outside Japan, was started in the first quality circle, outside Japan, was stated in the U.S.A. in 1974. In India, quality circles were first initiated by BHEL during 1980-81. Though quality circles were started in manufacturing organizations, they have now spread to other service sectors like banking, hospitals, transportation and education.

Quality control system must cover the systems and processes that underpin institutions' responsibilities for teaching and learning. The quality of education can be enhanced when administrators, teachers, staff and education board members develop new attitudes that focus on leadership, team work, cooperation, accountability and recognition.

Quality circle is a management concept primarily applied in the industrial sector. It is a group of 6-8 volunteers from the same area/department that meets regularly once a week, for an hour to solve work related problem. The members receive training in problem solving, statistical quality control, and group process. Quality circle recommends solution for quality and efficiency problems which the management may implement. A facilitator or a highly trained member helps to train circle member and ensures that things run smoothly.

Researchers find this concept to be beneficial for quality improvement because:

1. Everybody participates and contributes to the process of decision-making where problems are chosen, not given.
2. Quality circle help in building positive attitude.
3. Decision is by consensus, not by majority.
4. It is performance oriented, not problem focused.
5. Promotes prevention, not inspection.
6. Bring out extraordinary quality form ordinary people and
7. Recognizes and taps the intellectual potential of participants.

Features

- **Small Group of Employees:** The size of a quality circle is very important. The optimum number for members in a quality circle is about 8 to 10. If it is less than 5 then the group may lose vitality an may become inactive. Too large a group makes it difficult for everyone to participate. If the circle is more than 15 then there may not be active participation and may result in conflict.
- **Same work area:** The circle should comprise more or less a homogeneous group of people from same work area. They will usually have similar educational background, speak the same work language. The more homogeneous the group the more impressive will be its achievements and the greater its cohesion.
- **Voluntary:** This aspect makes quality circle a unique one. Members join voluntarily and no coercion or pressure is to be bought to join a quality circle. No one should be barred from becoming a member.
- **Meet regularly:** The circle should meet regularly. This will help in judging the efficiency of the circle.

- **Identify, Analyse and Evolve solution to work related problem:** The key area of concern for a quality circle is to identify analyse and solve work related problems. Personal grievances are not been tackled. They should present solutions to the management are implement solutions themselves.
- **Improvement in total performance:** Quality circles help in resolving work related problems. This, in turn, would enhance individual performance and total performance in the work area would improve.
- **Enrichment of work life:** Besides change in their performance, attitude, and behavior, quality circles would enrich the work life of the members. This would benefit the organization with overall productivity and efficiency.

Quality circles help in achieving and sustaining excellence leading to mutual benefit to employees as well as the organization. It is 'a way of capturing the creative and innovative power that lies within the workforce'.

It is widely recognized now that the concept of quality circle can be applied in institutions of higher education. It is a concept that is beneficial for quality improvement in higher education. Improving the quality of education; making education a better process of 'people building'; helping in self development, organizational development and eventually societal and national development, initiating total quality education (TQE), and building analytical minds so that people have a scientific approach to solving to solving problems are considered to be the primary objectives of introducing Quality Circles in institutions of higher education.

In the west, quality circles were implemented in a number of educational institutions. Central Piedmont Community College, Middlesex County College, and Lakeshare Technical Institute are some examples that stand out. In India, quality circles were introduced in some educational institutions recently. They include colleges in cities like Madurai, Bagalkot, Dharwad and Bangalore.

In Karnataka, the Department of Education, Government of Karnataka has taken initiatives for solving the problems related to quality of higher education through implementation of a programme of Total Quality Management. For this purpose, the government has established District Level Task Force (DLTF). The DLTF in different regions have implemented different approaches to improve the quality of higher education. Accordingly, it was decided to set up quality circles in all colleges with each teacher adopting 15-20 students and maintaining a record of academic counseling in the format prepared by the Department of Collegiate Education. Quality circles have been introduced in the education al field for the first time in Bagalkot district in Karnataka. To coordinate these activities these colleges have formed a separate quality assurance cell. The particulars related to the scheme of quality circles are as follows:

- **Quality assurance cell :** There are nine members in the quality assurance cell of an institution.
- **Convenor :** The principal of the college shall be the convenor of the quality assurance cell.
- **Resource Developer :** A member of the faculty shall function as a facilitator of Human Resource Department so as to organize learning and development programmers for all sections of the institution.
- **Academic Auditor :** A member of the teaching fraternity shall be responsible for auditing the academic activity including enhancement of intellectual inputs.
- **Infrastructure Planner :** This person shall be drawn from the management or member of the government body to plan and improve the infrastructure conditions including funding.

- **Extra Curricular Promoter :** A junior member of teaching staff shall plan and conduct extracurricular activity for all sections of the institutions individually and collectively.
- **Career Counsellor :** It shall be the responsibility of the member of the faculty to look after career guidance as well as placements.
- **Professional Counsellor** : A member of the faculty shall offer professional counseling to individual students.
- **Student's Voice :** This should be any student who may be invited by the Convenor independently or on a recommen-dation of one or more members of the quality assurance cell.
- **Objective of the Study** : The main aim of this study is to examine the internal processes of quality circles in higher education and their impact. The specific objectives of analysis in this paper include examining the internal process of functioning of these circles, analyzing the impact of quality circles on subjective measures such as student teacher relation, job/learning satisfaction, attitude towards group working and the overall perception of participating members about the quality circles.

A random sample of six colleges was selected out of 24 degree colleges in Bagalkot district of Karnatak University, which have been implementing quality circles for four years now. In the selected colleges, fifty quality circles were randomly selected out of 400 and 34 quality circles, which have been functioning. Ninety-two quality circle members were selected as individual respondents from the sampled quality circles.

For data collection four different questionnaires were designed. These consist of:

(*a*) *Institutional Profile* - to collect information about college

(*b*) *Circle Profile* - to collect information about quality circle (*c*) *Circle Process* - to collect information about operation of circle activities, and

(*d*) *Members' perception* about quality circle - to know the perception about functioning and effectiveness of quality circle.

To collect additional information, structured and semi-structured interviews mainly covered District Level Task Force members and District Level Quality Assurance Cell members. Semi-structured interviews were conducted involving principals, quality circle facilitators, leaders and members. Simple descriptive statistics such as mean, percentage and standard deviation were calculated by using statistical package for social science (SPSS) for analysis and interpretation of data.

Internal Dynamics of Quality Circles

The educational institutions covered in our study were found to have two variants of Quality Circles. One set of them are formed separately for teachers and students. And the other with teachers and students jointly. Irrespective of the nature of these quality circles, a majority of the members (58 per cent of teachers and 49 per cent of students) believe that improving the quality of education is the primary objective of quality circles. A good number of them (24 per cent of teachers and 40 per cent of students) also hold the view that quality circles are started for improving the performance of students. In any case the government's enthusiasm for encouraging teachers and students to involve better in different processes of educational system is clearly visible here. The DLTF has made it compulsory for all the government -aided colleges in the district to introduce quality circles.

Going by their origin and initial structure, quality circles will have to be voluntary endeavors of members. However, our study indicates that quality circles in educational institutions were not formed on a voluntary basis. Those becoming members voluntarily (40 per cent) do not constitute the majority. However, the response is to be still considered good since the concept of quality circle in educational institutions is still taking root. Suggestions and orientation from DLTF (36%), advice from teachers and peer level advice have made many students and teachers become members of quality circles. In many cases students from such circles because of the compulsion from their teachers. This has created disinterest for participation in circle activities. The pressing need for time mainly due to family compulsions and long durations of travel back home made it difficult for many members to voluntarily join quality circle movement. However. After joining and involving in its activities majority of such members have realized the value of the concept and could grasp the principle of the concept fast and hold a positive view of its need in educational institutions.

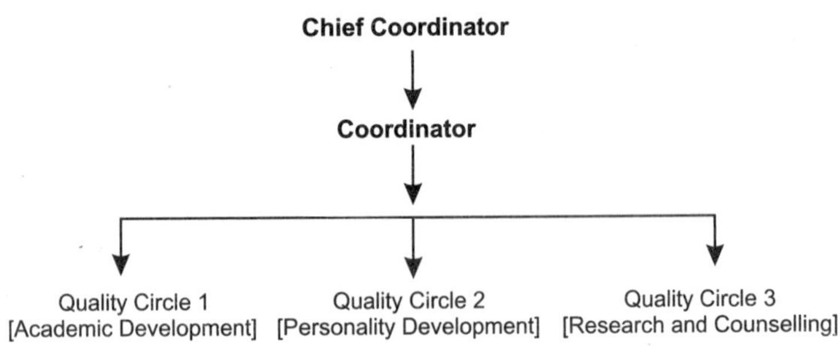

Fig. 5.1

Structure of Quality Circles

The colleges organize quality circles in the manner depicted in Fig. 5.1. This includes Chief Coordinator, Coordinator and quality circles at the college level and Convenor, leader and circles at the college level and Convenor, leader and circle members at each circle level. The chief coordinator and coordinator are the focal point or the central hub. Under their direction, policies and procedures for the programme are established and implemented. They then oversee the operation period. The position of chief coordinator and coordinator are normally held by the principal and a senior teacher of the college. The conveners are the liaison between the coordinator and circle leaders. They oversee and keep abreast of all activities within the circle for which they are responsible. Circle leaders are responsible for conducting meetings and coordinating the activities of the individual circle.

The scrutiny of the quality circle records in sampled institutions showed that major agenda for steering committee meetings were to establish long range plans for quality circle activities which aim at academic development, personality development research, counseling and review of the progress of the circle. From the interviews with the management, it emerged that they were concerned with the growth and proper functioning of quality circles. It was also found that the structure of all the quality circles is the same. This could be because of the fact that the DLTF has made uniformity in its implementation. In all institutions, it was reported that their management had been monitoring quality circle activities.

Quality Circle Meetings

The working of quality circles essentially revolve round their periodic meetings, where most of the quality issues are decided. Normally the quality circles were found to have a meeting of around 60 minutes (62%). The length of the meeting depends more on the involvement than on the number of items on the agenda. Quality circle meetings were generally held after working hours (92%). It is by its very nature that the activities of quality circles are not supposed to disturb the nor mal working hours. However, it is also a disadvantage since a good number of members are obviously eager to see off the meeting as early as possible to get back home. This feature is found in many circles in our study.

The frequency of quality circle meetings ranged from one meeting per month to one meeting per week. However, a majority of the institutions had scheduled quality circle meeting every week (59%). It is reported that quality circle members used to forget to attend the meetings. During the discussions with quality circle members, it emerged that initially members used to find it difficult to keep track of meeting dates. It was then planned that quality circle groups should follow a practice of meeting every week at a definite time and place. Since then the meetings take place normally as per schedule. However, the attendance of the members in the meeting varies from 25 per cent to 100 per cent though average attendance seems to be at an acceptable level, these meetings have not become an attraction for members to attend.

The study found that training in problem solving techniques like brain storming, pare to diagram, cause and effect diagram is extensive (25%), adequate (45%). It is also found that such efforts were totally missing in some (7%) cases. It is found that quality circle facilitators and leaders were trained by external and/or internet trainer. During the discussion, it was reported that students were eager to receive training rather than teachers. It is interesting to note that training is one of the weak links in these institutions and enough important has to be given to educate both teachers and students. Moreover, training has not benefited the teachers much and they are also not interested in receiving training programmes. This could be because the training programmes. This could be because the training programmes are held somewhere outside the campus and college managements were not permitting them to attend these programmes.

Facilities such as meeting room, furniture, blackboard and stationary are a must for every quality circle. It is learnt that out of six colleges only three were providing these facilities. The colleges have created quality circles but support for their activities is not easily coming forth. Many members feel that since the meetings of quality circles are generally held would need light refreshments during the meeting, but there is no provision for that. Similarly many of them feel that by the time they assemble for the meeting they- would be tired and quality circle meetings add to their strain and they cannot be really productive.

The internal dynamics of quality circles in our study reveals that the circles have been established through external impetus than internal realization. No doubt there are many active groups and a good deal of brain-storming has been taking place. It is giving a good platform for students and teachers to assemble in an informal setting and exchange ideal. However, these groups have not evolved as a cultural formation and hence members fail to identify themselves as an integral part of the group. The expectation of members that they are essentially helping the college management, and, therefore, the management should make some provisions for the working of circles is an indication that quality circles here are not evolved structures but implanted ones.

Impact of Quality Circles

Our study tried to ascertain the specific gains through quality circles, especially to its members. The perception of participating members, in terms of what have they gained over a period of time.

The teachers also felt that quality circles have helped them improve their communication ability, team spirit and has given them an opportunity to use their knowledge and skill, which will not find enough use in their routine work. During the interview the students reported higher personal benefits (in particular, confidence building and personality development) as a result of quality circle activities than the teachers.

During personal discussions, the teachers reported that they got really involved while participating in the quality circle activities especially when they were able to think of a solution to the problem over which they were stuck for long. Some of the very positive views expressed by teacher members include yes, quality circle activities have aided in increasing work place interaction, there is improved efficiency "the quality circle activities have made the college a happier place', and 'education and learning has become more meaningful and enjoyable process". We have also used some objective measures to know the impact of quality circles in the colleges. Some such measures are presented in the Table 5.1.

TABLE 5.1 : Objective Measures of Functioning Quality Circles

Particulars	*Average*
Average Age of Quality Circle	5.5 years
Average No. of Problems identified	2
Average No. of Suggestions made	3.8
Average of Regularity of meetings	80%
Average of Regularity of attendance	80%
Average of suggestions accepted by Management	0.66

It may be seen that on an average the quality circles have been fairly regular in terms of their meetings and attendance in meetings. On an average 2 problems were identified and 3.8 suggestions made by each Quality Circles. The percentage of acceptance of suggestions by the college management (average of 2.66) is also quite good. This shows that the quality circles have been quite practical in their approach and have succeeded in giving concrete suggestions to college managements.

Specific case studies of some colleges and some select quality circles have revealed that the circle activities have been of particular help to students. In one case the discussions in quality circle meetings have lead to teachers' circles engaging in counseling students. This helped students in selecting the course of study, elective papers and career options based on their interest and ability.

In another case, the third grade students of a particular class were divided and formed into small groups for the purpose of study. Instead of keeping them all at the same level of learning.

In one of the colleges a quality circle conducted the audit of the procedure followed in the library for numbering, stacking and distribution of books. Based on its suggestions the system was remodelled and everyone found it convenient and efficient. One of the circles (involving both teachers and students) had made an audit of the consumption of electrical power in the college and recommended a number of energy saving practices. After implementing these practices the college could achieve a 20 per cent reduction in electricity consumption in the very first year.

TABLE 6.2 : Gains of participation of QC activities as perceived by Quality Circle Members (Average Scores of Teachers and Students)

Gains	*Teachers*	*Students*	*Total*
Ability to use knowledge	4.21	4.04	4.125
Recognition	4.06	4.22	4.14
Job/learning satisfaction	4.13	4.05	4.09
Improvement of communication	4.41	4.18	4.295
Team spirit	4.35	4.24	4.295
Participation in group discussion	4.01	3.93	3.97
Public speaking skill	3.92	3.90	3.91
Individual improvement	3.96	3.86	3.91
Proud of being QC member	4.23	4.32	4.275
Recommendation to others for joining QC	4.13	4.23	4.18
Overall Score	3.93	4.22	4.05

The above findings (Table 6.2) reveal that quality circles have indeed made a qualitative change in the learning processes in many colleges, the college management, the teachers. The college management, the teachers and the students have all gained through this experiment. However, there have been problems as well. There has been resistance to stating of quality circles and for the activities of these circles from different comers. The resistance level seems to be quite high from the teachers' side. Many of them feel that it is an additional and unnecessary burden on them and most of the work of the quality circle work have to be actually handled by them. The college management in many cases is not interested in this since they are compelled to provide additional facilities.

In some cases the quality circle (QC) meetings have raised some very real but embarrassing issues for the teachers and college managements and they have closed down the circles. Even though the students have not understood the concept very well, generally the resistance level form them is not much. Wherever the circles have done well, the participation and contribution of students in those circles have been exemplary.

The overall influence of quality circles is more visible among students (average 4.22) than teachers (3.93). This could be because the teachers by virtue of their profession and experience already have exposure to some kind of personality development course but the students being inexperienced got an exposure of this magnitude probably for the first time in their life and so were more influenced. Even though the concept has been brought into the educations as a part of the state intervention as a part of the state intervention towards quality improvement, the quality circles are definitely relevant. Its objective and the voluntary participative processes need to be appreciated by all concerned.

Suggestions

Having seen the experience of colleges under study implementing the scheme of Quality Circles, the following suggestions seem to be worth considering.

- The environment for implementation of quality circle is of utmost importance. An environment of trust and mutual faith can give the quality circles stronger moorings whereas half hearted efforts with an eye on the results and environment of suspicion can destroy quality circles.
- An appropriate system for recognizing and rewarding the quality circle activities needs to be designed and implemented. The quality circle activities should be given wide publicity through in-house magazines and notice boards.
- Adequate support and appropriate implementation measures of the programme are crucial for successful

quality circles. The management ought to create awareness about the quality circle concept for the entire staff. Management should take care that participants do not perceive the concept as imposed, since the voluntary nature of the concept of vital importance.

- Educators tend to emphasize individual achievement and personal importance, which may run contrary to quality circle progress. Most quality problems are built into the system and the system can be improved only when it is previewed from a prevention mindset rather than an inspection mindset. If quality circles are to work, they must have the long term devotion of the teachers and institutions.

Though originally intended for industry, the quality circle clearly has uses in education. It is rightly said, 'longest voyage starts with the first step'. The colleges in Bagalkot district have made the right beginning through the inception of quality circles and they are of significance. Those colleges seeking to improve employee and student morale and to provide quality education through participatory management technique may well wish to learn more about the quality circle, its success, and its effects capabilities of the organisation and to deal with all emerging challenges. Further the labour had very less bargaining power in the market and it is the most unpredictable and sensitive and capable of adjusting to environment. In order to enhance the profitability efficiency and overall organisational effectiveness. The labour which is competitive, sensitive, flexible and capable of adjusting to any environment needs to be trained properly keeping in mind the goals of organisation.

Higher Education in 'Trishanku' —A Study

—G. Chandrayya*

Introduction

The higher education systems in many countries today are at the cross-roads. There is a gradual shift from education being a state responsibility to its privatisation. Many consider the public sector to be inefficient in the field of education and correspondingly the private sector as efficient and therefore desirable. Nevertheless, the case for public provisioning of education remains strong. It is imperative for the state to play a dominant role in this field.

The value of higher education was recognized in traditional societies perhaps much more than in modern societies. Though no attempts were made to identify and quantify the benefits of education, the value of education was rarely questioned. Education and knowledge were viewed as great wealth in themselves, besides being sources of an increase in wealth. It seems that even the existence of externalities was acknowledged in traditional societies, both in the ancient and modern periods. Accordingly, societies invested resources in education voluntarily and gladly, and many a time without expecting any direct economic return. Even in modern societies for a long time, say, until the advent of the 1970s, it had been so. It was held that the benefits of

*Reader in Commerce, Government College (A), Rajahmundry, A.P.

education were vast and widespread, and in the long run, government investments made in education could be recovered by society through the increased productivity of the labour force and through consequent higher tax receipts by the government, and hence there was no need for any specific measures directly to recover the investments made in education from students or from any non-governmental sources. As observed, "[higher] education is an investment and will pay for itself; and will increase the earnings of the beneficiary students and the government will recover its costs through consequent higher tax receipts".

The immediate post-war period in Europe and the post-Independence period in developing countries was dominated by a welfare state philosophy and a philosophy of social democratic consensus. It was strongly felt that government could do almost everything for everybody. Following John Maynard Keynes, the power of the state was recognized-planning, provision, financing and other interventions by the State were favoured and an extension of the traditional functions of the State was promoted. Education had been one important sector in which the role of the State had been recognised widely. The importance of public education was highlighted earlier in classical political economy also. There is a long and honourable tradition from Adam Smith to Alfred Marshall which assigns to publicly supported education a major role not only in promoting social peace and harmony, and self-improvement, but in the process of wealth-creation itself. Accordingly, a gold standard tradition was established characterized by state provision and financing of education.

The advent of the 1970 heralded a continuing financial crisis in education. The crisis was characterised by high rates of inflation, shrinking public budgets for education along with increasing student numbers, declining per student expenditures, extremely inadequate investment in the quality of education, severe distortions in inter-sectoral and intra-sectoral allocation of resources, widening of inter-country and intra-country inequalities in expenditure on education, etc.

Since the beginning of the 1980s, modern neo-liberal economic reform policies have been unveiled in several developing countries in the form of stabilisation and adjustment reform programmers, associated with the International Monetary Fund and the World Bank. The economic reform policies of the Bretton Wood institutions and privatisation are rightly felt to be synonymous by many. Rather privatisation or a movement towards privatisation has become the most significant agenda of the Bank. The underlying philosophy of these policies is that any aspect related to the public sector is inefficient, and any aspect related to the private sector is, *ipso facto,* efficient and desirable. All this led to the eclipse of Keynesianism in the mid-1970s, and gradually and reluctantly paved the way for the entry of market principles. The concept of free market used in modern economics until the end of 1970s or early 1980s was probably consistent with an appropriate role of the government to take care of market failures. This was the basis of welfare economics. But the 1980s and 1990s brought about a complete swing of the pendulum in which social democratic values and welfare state concerns were replaced by the free market philosophy that stresses individual economic values and gains. Individual freedom and choice are preferred to social (or public) choice. According to the somewhat extreme form of free market philosophy, there is no meaning to 'social good' and 'social welfare' there is no such thing as society or value to society that is inseparable from individual gains. Only individuals are real, and their gains are crucially important and individual freedom is more important than even democratic values. Public good and social justice are viewed as impossible and even as not necessarily desirable.

The shift in development paradigm is taking place all over. Many countries, particularly developing countries are in transition. The transition is from a development paradigm that was predominantly based on Keynesianism to a 'neo-liberal' paradigm. Markets more clearly the private sector, now holds the centre stage. It is argued increasingly nowadays that it is not the government, but the market that can do everything for everybody.

This philosophy entered the education sector as well more strongly the education sector as well more strongly the higher education sector. Correspondingly a reduced role of the state in education, more explicitly higher education, is promoted as an economically and educationally efficient proposal and it is argued that the role of the government should be confined broadly to the formulation of a coherent policy framework. The creeping in of a market philosophy into education which is much more ingrained in the American psyche has come as something of a culture shock not only to most people in developing countries, but also to several European countries, including the UK and has resulted in several kinds of tensions and conflicts. Privatisation is being pursued in higher education as a very effective measure of improving efficiency and as an important measure of financial crisis.

Thus, today we notice that higher education systems in many countries - developing as well as developed are at the crossroads; Traditionally higher education is viewed as one that creates and diffuses knowledge. Rather expansion of frontiers of knowledge is regarded as the most important function of education. Many societies assigned high value to know ledge for the sake of knowledge, as knowledge was considered wealth. Secondly higher education was viewed as an instrument of personal development of individuals, expanding intellectual horizons of the individuals, their interests and potential and empowering the individuals to have better quality of life, as contemporary sociologists and psychologists argue. Thirdly, higher education was viewed as an instrument of social engineering, socializing individuals to the values of the society - social, ethical, cultural and political, so that societies become more virtuous with more and more people who have had access to higher education (a lasociologists like Durkheim), Lastly, the human capital theorists placed emphasis on the role of education in transformation of human beings into human capital, an instrument of production and economic growth and thereby economic well-being of the people and societies. Many institutions of higher education in the contemporary period aimed at serving all these functions Thus, it is long held that higher education institutions have social functions; they possess important social, cultural as well as economic roles; they provide public service, they are different form commercial and business orgnisations, they produce human capital, and even specialized human capital; and that their output is not necessarily tangible, and above all, they are not for profit institutions.

Now with the unveiling of the economic reform policies, the role of higher education is being reinterpreted and redefined. The market-promoting polices everywhere pose serious challenges to higher education. New values, policies and practices and practices replaced traditional and well-established values, concepts and approaches. Social democratic visions are being replaced by market-driven policies. 'Marketisation' has become the buzzword. The role of the government is being 'reinvented'. Their traditional functions of production and dissemination of knowledge are under attack. Public subsidization of higher education is being increasingly criticised. Equity in higher education is no more cared for. The modern economic policies, or simply called the market reforms that aim at making higher education institutions responsive to market forces do not distinguish between education and any commercial product.

This chapter presents an analytical account of some of the prominent emerging trends in higher education, and describes how higher education is moving from state to market, and the costes involved therein.

State versus Markets in Higher Education[1]

Generally education is publicly provided by very nation. Dominance of the state subsidies in an outstanding feature of most education systems. Such a unique positions is shared only by a very limited range of goods and services such as national defence, internal security, courts, police, etc. Even in those cases, where education is not publicly provided, it is subsidized by the state. Education, including higher education, is heavily subsidized by the state in almost all the countries of the world not only in developing countries, but also in developed countries. Conventionally why has education been given such a treatment? There seems to exist a powerful persuasive economic logic and a social, political and historical rationale for this.

Case for Role of State in Higher Education

There are several arguments in the literature that justify the role of the state in higher education: education is a public good; and higher education at least a quasi public good producing a wide variety and huge magnitude of externalities. Consumers of education confer external benefits on those not acquiring education. The social benefits of having a large population which has had access to higher education go beyond the increase in GNP. It is also argued that social benefits if education cannot be reduced to individual self-interest. Hence by taxing those who receive these benefits and subsidizing the provision of education, the welfare of both groups, and thereby the society as a whole, can be improved. The externalities include improvement in health, reduction in population growth, reduction in poverty, improvement in income distribution, reduction in crime, rapid adoption of new technologies, strengthening of democracy, ensuring of civil liberties, etc, and even dynamic externalities and 'technological' externalities, which are necessary for technical progress and economic growth and to arrest diminishing marginal returns. These positive externalities constitute a powerful justification for the state to play a crucial role in education. The externalities or the 'uncompensated' benefits from education are regarded to be legion. Further, when democracy, reduction of crime, economic growth, redistribution of resources, etc, are viewed as other public goods, it is important to note that education helps in their fulfilment.

A similar aspect is that education is also a 'merit good'. It is a merit good, consumption of which needs to be promoted, people could be ignorant of the benefits of education, or may not be appreciative of value of education, or may not be able to foresee the implications of their investment decisions in education, and may be unwilling to invest in education. But governments are expected to have better information than individuals or families, and should be wiser and more able to look into the future and accordingly take wise decisions regarding investment in education. The important aspect is that not the others, but the individual recipient himself/herself benefits to a greater extent than he/she is aware of. For instance, the effect of education on wages may be known, but the likely impact on productivity in general, on family health and nutrition, ability to make decisions regarding one self, or about his/her family members relating to education, employment, etc. is less likely to be anticipated and under stood. In other words, it is highly implausible to argue that individuals can be represented as economic agents who can be relied on. To make choices that are in all cases cases rational; or that or are infinitely clear headed about how to go about realising their goals, and that they are capable of foreseeing all of the consequences of their actions, and can discover which is the best strategy to service their chosen ends. It is widely held that governments would be wiser than the individuals in understanding the implications of investing in education. Consumer ignorance is a typical case that necessitates public subsidization.

Thirdly, state provision of higher education is advocated on the grounds of providing equality of opportunity. Ensuring equality of opportunity in education to everyone irrespective of not only social, racial, and cultural background, but also economic background is considered an important function of the modern state. It is held for a long time and by many that "it is necessary to provide free education at all levels and also to subsidies students living expenses in post-secondary schooling so as to guarantee equality of educational opportunity". Education is found to be an effective instrument of equity. In the absence of state subsidies, only those who could afford to pay would enroll in schools. The concern for equality of opportunity has led to almost universal agreement that the government should subsidise that the government should subsidise education.

A strong, argument accepted by many in support of state funding of higher education is the existence of imperfections in capital markets. As researcher observed, imperfections in capital markets and asymmetric information are possible justifications for the public subsidization of higher education. In several developing countries markets are 'incomplete' and credible markets do not exist. Education credit markets are also incomplete, imperfect capital markets inhibit students from borrowing against the uncertain future returns of higher education. Problems of offering human capital as collateral, lead to under-investment in education, especially among the poor families. People may not prefer to borrow to invest in education. The gestation period of which is relatively very long, and may not be ready to take risk of investing in education, the benefits of which are not certain. Risk associated with human capital investments could be difficult to diversify and could be very high to the society. For the individual the risk of not completing a given level of education, or facing the risk of falling market value of his/her education are indeed high. Even more importantly. The lenders would be understandably reluctant to accept risk backed only by uncertain future incomes of the reluctant debtors. Hence the need for state subsidies.

Fifthly, education is a sector, which is subject to economies of scale, or increasing returns to scale. Average costs of providing education declines as enrolments increase. If a production process is characterized with decreasing average cost condition, it may be more efficient for government to operate this process. Further, higher levels of education can be particularly subject to this phenomenon. University systems, scientific equipment, libraries, etc, cannot be used on a small scale. Hence it may be more efficient for government to provide it. So government monopoly of education, including higher education, is viewed desirable, compared to allowing many providers in the field.

Arguments Against Role of the State

Of late several questions are being raised on the rational of state subsidies in general and subsidisation of education in particular, and within education, more particularly higher education. The several arguments against public subsidisation of education are essentially of three kinds: efficiency arguments, equity arguments, and pragmatic considerations. First, much opposition to public subsidisation of education, has emerged from estimates of rates of return to education. The social rates of return are found to be consistently lower than private rates of return to education, and hence it was recommended that public subsidies could be reduced, and individuals could be asked to pay for their education.

Secondly, it is argued that public subsidization of education produces perverse effects on distribution. It is argued that public subsidization of education, especially higher education, would be regressive, increasing income inequalities by transferring the resources from the poor to the rich, as the education (particularly but not exclusively higher education) subsidies accrue more to the rich than to the poor. Reduction in education subsidies in general is also advocated arguing that education subsidies could be targeted to the poor only [World Bank 1994].

Thirdly, governments in developing countries are increasingly facing a resource crunch. Economic reform policies adopted in many developing countries, including stabilization and structural adjustment policies also necessitate cuts in public expenditures across the board. Education is viewed as one sector, where state can with draw rather relatively easily.

There are also several other arguments. Public subsidisation is not needed to promote equity or to promote democracy.

It is also contended that with heavy subsidization by the state, education institutions become vulnerable to government control: it is inefficient to give subsidies (in the form of grants to institutions) since it offers no incentives to allocate the resources efficiently: it may not be desirable to subsidise higher education. While basic needs such as basic education and health care are not adequately funded; in other words, public resources get misallocated, etc.

It is also felt that reduction in the role of the state and in state and in state subsidies would not adversely affect the growth of higher education, as cost recovery measures can be adopted. Since education, particularly higher education may not be price-elastic, it is believed that cost recovery measures would not lead to any significant fall in enrolments; on the other hand, cost recovery measures would improve access, and also would lead to also would lead to improvement in quality of education on the one hand, and making students more diligent about studies on the other. Given the high private rates of return, people will be willing to pay for education.

Assessment of Arguments

The debate between the two sides, state versus markets, or familiarly known as liberal versus neo-liberal groups, is intensifying in the recent years. How far are the arguments and counter arguments valid? it may be noted that all arguments against the role of the state cannot necessarily be considered as those in favour of markets in higher education. Secondly, some of the arguments against the role of the state assume that the level of efficiency of the state sector is given and there is no scope for improvement in the same, which is not true. While it may be possible to marshal enough evidence to argue on either side, there are some aspects that stand out very clearly in favour of a dominant role of the state in higher education, which are rarely questioned. For example, even those who oppose pubic subsidization of higher education recognize that it produces large externalities.[2] Even researcher implicitly agreed that because of externalities the associated with education it should be publicly financed. Though all the social benefits cannot be identified and measured accurately, there is still a consensus that they are substantial. The other aspects widely shared are: education as a public good (and quasi-public good in case of higher education) merit good nature, education as social investment, market imperfections, and economies of scale. Further, many arguments made against public subsidization do not have unqualified support either from theory or empirical evidence. Based on sound economic reasoning, researcher concluded, "publicly financed education is a legitimate end of public activity, even to extreme exponents of classical' economic doctrine".

The case against public subsidies in education in the recent years is based the premise that governments in developing countries do not have adequate resources at their disposal, and that the scope for restructuring the public budgets, and thereby increasing the subsidies substantially to education is rather limited. This is not an argument per se against public subsidization or in favour of markets. Except quoting the figures relating to budget deficits, or those relating to external indebtedness, and the corresponding debt service charges of the developing countries, this premise has rarely been critically examined. Arguments are made for restructuring public budgets by withdrawing resources from unproductive sectors and their reallocation towards education. Some research also exists that shows that education expenditures are effected by military expenditures, indicating a clear trade-off between public expenditures on defence and education patterns of public expenditures in developing countries also show that the governments are not as much starved of resources will, especially in case of sectors like education.

There is a general argument that higher education subsidies are regressive. It is also stated, that subsidies to higher education accrue to the better-off sections of the society, while those to primary education accrue to the masses. It is argued that public subsidization of education produces perverse effects on distribution, a finding that was proved wrong. Researcher has concluded in a cross -country analysis. "There is little evidence in favour of the postulate of a significant disequalising effect of public subsidy to higher education. If there is such an effect at all. It appears to be stronger in the DCs than in the LDCs" (developed countries than in less developed countries). The public subsidization of education would even correct distortions in taxation and hence it is efficient to subsidise education. In a careful review of several studies, and after standardizing their results, found that higher education in most cases does contribute to progressivity and moreover that when the analytical methods employed are most advanced, progressivity is found without exception." It is also widely shared that any withdrawal of public subsidies would certainly make the system worse, more regressive. Further, it is also noted that markets are cumulatively and inherently inegalitarian in relation to the distribution of resources in society. As researcher demonstrates, it may be justified to tax the poor to finance higher education of even the rich, because of the externalities associated with higher education (of the rich), which can be relatively rich in a permanent income sence, the poor (or less able) also realize a portion of the gains from the rich (or more able) receiving higher education.

It is also recognized that state subsidies need not necessarily be regressive *per se.* it depends upon the nature, type and kind of subsidies. For instance, if subsidies that are expected to be universally available to all are targeted, orvice it may produce adverse effects. The type of subsidies, e.g. grants to institutions versus grants to students, may also matter in this context. It is also felt the solution to regressive effects of subsidies lies in progressive taxation system, rather than in eliminating or reducing subsidies.

The use of the estimates on rates of return to education in support of arguments against public subsidies is also found to be not proper. First, the high levels of private rates of return may not even sustain themselves for long, as already experienced by some countries. Reducing the students' willingness to pay. Secondly, private rates of return will decline if public subsidies are drastically reduced or altogether withdrawn, making investment in education unattractive from individual point of view. Thirdly and more importantly, it is now well noted that the social rates of return to education are not true social returns: except for tax benefits, no other social benefits are considered in the estimation of social rates of return to education.

Hence, it is contended that rates of return cannot be used to argue against public subsidies or even for any sound public policy on education. Further, properly estimated social returns could be much higher than not only the earlier estimates on social rates of return. But also higher than the private rates of return.

There are also a few who feel that education may not qualify to become a public good, as the criteria of 'non-exclusion' and the 'free-rider' do not apply. It is mentioned that one's admission to a school may mean denial to somebody else, as the number of places in schools could be restricted. What is important, is to check the applicability of the criteria of non-exclusion and free rider not to consumption of the service (admission in school), but to receipt of the benefits of education. After all, people who have not gone to schools cannot be excluded from getting benefits of having educated population in the neighbourhood.

Lastly, it has to be noted that many of those who argue for increased cost recovery in higher education do not oppose public subsidization per se; on the other hand, since there is "limited scope for increased public spending", it is argued that additional resources can be mobilized through a variety of measures. They also recognize that public subsidies can increase efficiency. Hence the real need to raise resources by the state through tax and non-tax revenues.

As researcher summed up long ago, market failures - consumer ignorance, technical economies of scale, economies of scale, externalities in production and in consumption, public good, and inherent imperfections in capital and insurance markets - inhibit the attainment of Pareto optimality in education investments. In case of higher education, researcher agrees that of the above, externalities and imperfections in capital and insurance markets are relevant. Hence the government has to subsidise education. Governments subsidise education, not just for efficiency, but also for reasons of equity, and various other social and political objectives. Hence, as observed, even if theoretical justification is weak, "it would probably be a mistake to curtail sharply public subsidies to education". To conclude, there is not much disagreement on the rationale of the role of the state and state funding of higher education. The opposition to a publicly-financed system is a political opposition to paying taxes rather than an attitude ineluctably derived from the mainstream of economic reasoning.

Current Trends towards Marketisation

Despite the abundant knowledge on the importance of the role of the state, higher education systems are in transition. The economic reform policies introduced in almost all developing countries during the last quarter of the century, required (*a*) a drastic cut in public expenditures across the board, including higher education, and (*b*) promotion of markets in higher education. And on the whole, higher education suffered severely. Public expenditure on higher education declined in many developing countries-in terms of relative priorities (proportion of GNP or of total government expenditure that is allocated to higher education), and/or in public expenditure on higher education in absolute terms in real prices (and sometimes even in nominal prices)—total as well as per student. Noticeable cuts could also be noted in several countries, specifically in public expenditure on quality and equity related inputs in higher education (*e.g.*, research, and scholarships). Recovery of costs of higher education from the students (in the form of high and even full cost-equivalent fees) has been an important strategy adopted in most countries, along with raising of resources from other non-governmental sources including industry, by forging close university-industry links.

Along with these and the public apathy for higher education, one can note a strong emergence of forces in favour of private higher education. The lack of resources is one oft-cited reason for the growth of private higher education. But an equally important reason is the change in attitudes towards higher education, and towards private higher education, and towards 'for profit' private institutions of higher education, in particular. The public and merit good nature of higher education is being increasingly discounted. Private higher education is projected as an efficient system that can improve access and quality as well as equity!

Governments have either implicitly encouraged higher education institutions to adopt market relevant policies, or explicitly formulated policies that contribute to rapid privatization of higher education. Such policies include withdrawal of government grants and incentives to mobilize financial resources from non-governmental sources, including fees and others, introduction of 'marketable' courses of study that can be 'sold' to the students in place of long-term courses of study, appointment of industrialists as heads and/or chairpersons of governing bodies of higher education institutions. Management, financial management including cost recovery and profit/surplus-marking, have become the traits that are looked for in such appointments. The march towards marketisation of higher education is taking place through a variety of measures: financial privatization of public universities, transfer of ownership of public institutions and establishment of private institutions private institutions with government support, self-financing private institutions (with no government support), and profit making private institutions-all focusing on short-term market considerations and immediate market relevance. The emerging private institutions also consist more of institutions without government recognition. Universities also began to transform themselves into 'entrepreneurial universities' and autonomy from the government has also become a buzzword. The purpose of the universities, their ownership, sources of revenue, norms of management, and the role of the government in university development have been changing very fast. The changes are not confined to newly established institutions, but even the universities established several decades, if not centuries ago are affected by these changes, and there is a steady march form publicness to high privateness in higher education. As Johnstone (1999) described, the progress towards 'high privateness' in higher education (shown in table 1) is very fast.

The emerging scenario depicts varying degrees of privatization of higher education. First, an 'extreme' version of privatization of higher education, colleges and universities being managed and funded by the private sector, with little government intervention. Second, there is 'strong' degree of privatisation, which means recovery of full costs of public higher education from users-students, their employers or both. Third. There is a moderate form of privatisation implying public provision of higher education but with a reasonable level of financing from non-governmental sources. Lastly, there is what can be termed 'pseudo-privatisation', which cannot be really called privatization; institutions offering higher education under this category are privately managed but government-aided. They were originally created by private bodies, but receive nearly the whole of their expenditure from governments. All types and forms of privatisation seem to take place rapidly in many developing countries without any coherent perspective and plan, producing different kinds of problems.

On the whole, one can summarise the emerging trends and changing public policies in higher education in many developing countries that are in transition. These trends are not exhaustive; they are only indicative. The features listed under the two categories, *viz.*, 'conventional system' and 'emerging system' includes some of the changes that have already taken place in some countries, those that are slowly taking place in some other countries. And those that are taking place very fast in a few others. However, neither of the two systems is final in any sense.

Entrepreneurial Universities

In short, the emerging higher education system can be summed up as a transformation of academic institutions into "entrepreneurial universities" and "commercial institutions", the single most important objective of which seems to be mobilization of more and more resources. The "higher education bazaar" is growing every where in developed as well as developing countries with all its ugly faces.

The emerging private-moderate or highly private or predominantly private higher education systems are found to be creating serious problems in terms of access, quality and equity in higher education. Earlier reviews have exploded several myths about the superiority of private higher education. For example, it was shown that the higher quality of private education compared with public higher education was exaggerated; the graduates from private universities do not necessarily receive higher rewards in the labour market in the form of lower unemployment rates, better paid jobs and consequently higher earnings; rather external efficiency of private higher education is not higher than public higher education: the private sector does not respond rightly to the economic needs of the individual and society, if at all it does, it responds to short-term needs of the markets: very rarely private enterprises have genuine philanthropic motives in opening private universities, and in general such institutions tend to become profit-making institutions; private institutions create in equalities in education and in society; and private institutions are also not necessarily a political.

Developing countries require a rapid growth of good quality higher education for their very survival in the highly competitive globalised world. Some have argued that a threshold level of gross enrolment ratio in higher education is about 20 per cent. Only those countries that could have such a ratio, could become economically advanced and vice versa. It is also important to note that only those societies that have developed their public higher education systems could economically progress; and those countries that have expanded their higher education systems depending on private sector, or what can be called, 'predominantly' private higher education systems, could not progress much. For instance, most of the countries in South America could reach a gross enrolment ratio of above 20 per cent in higher education, but they continue to remain developing counties.

The problem is essentially the interests of the market forces (private universities) and those state universities are different. The former may even conflict not only with academic interests but also with national interests. As a result, protecting the research culture becomes a big challenge.

The conflicting interests of the state and the markets in education are so serious, that any attempt to forge a partnership between the two may be counter productive. In fact, there are some who advocate a middle path-state-market partnership or public-private partnerships in higher education. This, which was described as 'welfare pluralism' represents a middle ground, a centrist position, in the balance between the public and the private, the state and the non -state sectors. It rests on the following premises:

"(*a*) that the limitations and limits of state owned welfare— fiscal and administrative should be clearly recognized;

(*b*) that the state cannot and should not be the monopoly or near-monopoly provider of social welfare;

(*c*) that non-state providers can and should play a bigger part in the supply, and especially delivery, of services; and (*d*) that the move from a state- centred welfare towards welfare pluralism could result in greater inequality in the distribution of social benefits but that this is unavoidable".

But such a middle path is also not found to be really a middle path, as the power of the market forces is tremendous, and once unleashed, they are not likely to be easily regulated. What they can do, can hardly be undone and these forces cannot be regulated. As a result, the middle path eventually converges with the total market system, reminding the familiar 'The Arab and the Camel' story.

Summary and Concluding Observations

Education is a state function in almost all countries of the world. This is not confined to basic education. Even higher education. Including higher technical and professional education, is heavily subsidised by the state not only in the economies where development policies tilt explicitly in favour of welfare and equity, but also in the developed market economies. Traditionally, the role of the state has been justified by the recognition of educations capable of education as capable of producing externalities, as a public good (and as a quasi-public good in case of higher education), as a merit good, as a social investment for human development, and as a major instrument of equity, besides as a measure of quality of life in itself.

It is also well noted that markets cannot ensure optimum supply of education, and that left to the individuals or the market mechanism, social investment would be below optimum or socially desirable levels. The quality of education offered in many private universities was found to be below the normal level and the marketing methods adopted by some institutions were beneath the dignity of a true university and even of a good market.

Even when markets work well and students receive quality service, private institutions may still fail to serve the public interest. But in the current wave of market reforms, questions are being raised on the role of the state and on the rationale of public subsidies, and it is also being indicated that it is both desirable and feasible to reduce, if not eliminate altogether, the public subsidies in higher education. This paper has presented a review of some of these argument being made in favour of the state versus markets and restated how important it is for the state to continue to play a critical role in higher education. It is argued that any significant reduction in the role of the state in higher education is neither feasible nor desirable.

To conclude, essentially due to the critical role played by the developing countries earlier and still in the advanced counties, today higher education is no more elitist; it is somewhat 'democratised' with a large proportion of socio-economic weaker sections participating in higher education. This also helped in attaining self-reliance in manpower needs of the economy (*e.g.*, India). Secondly, higher education is rightly and increasingly viewed as an if not the only, effective instrument of socio-economic mobility of the weaker sections of the society. Thirdly, it is also widely recognized that higher education is an recognized that higher education is an important factor of economic growth, and it is education that makes the basic difference between the developed and the developing countries. All this viewed in the broad context of relatively low levels of living of the people, and imperfect and incomplete markets, and given other sociopolitical considerations, makes it imperative on the part of the state to play a dominant role in the provision of higher education and to yield no place to market mechanisms in higher education.

REFERENCES

1. Arrow, Kenneth J. (1993): Excellence and Equity in Higher Education, *Education Economics* 1(1): 5-12.
2. Blaug, Mark (1983): Declining Subsidies to Higher Education: An Economic Analysis In: H Giersch (ed), *Reassessing the Role of Government in the Mixed Economy*, Kiel: Instiut fur Welt Wirtschaft,

pp. 125-35 [reprinted in Blaug, (ed), *The Economics of Education and the Education of an Economist*, Aldershot: Edward Elgar, (1987): pp. 227-43].

3. Blaug, Mark and Maureen Woodhall (1979): Patterns of Subsidies to Higher Education in Europe, *Higher Education* (November 7 : Sepplement): 331-61.
4. Bok, Derek (2003): *Universities in the Market Place : The Commercialisation of Higher Education*. Princeton University Press, Princeton.

New Techniques in the Development of Human Resource after Globalisation

—*Dr. D. Tata Rao**

—*Roopesh K. Misra***

Human resources are the life of knowledge industry. Due to ever growing demand for manpower, the human resource department in any organisation faces never ending pressure to attract, retain and motivate the best in the industry. Satisfied employees are true "Brand ambassadors" of the organisation which shapes is image among the potential employees in the job industry. Employee development and retention plays a pivotal role in growth of an organisation.

In order to give a "breakthrough" on account of "break-down" employees aptitude and commitment are essential. Mentorship will positively help to retain and to improve employees commitment, contribution, and aptitude and encourages employees continuity. A good practice of HRD is essential now a days to enhance competence, commitment and culture. In order to give all Organisations its winning edge the HR today is expected to comprehend, innovative, and sustain relevant strategies and contribute effectively to the organization.

Every organization is consisting of people, process and purpose. Though human resource is the driving force but not given adequate significance and always put behind the scene.

---

*Reader in Commerce, Government Degree College, Yelamanchili, Vishakhapatnam, A.P.

**Manager at Mumbai.

In all organisations human resources shapes the organisation from scratch to the pinnacle of success. It is important to note here that the "most important resource of our organisation is human resource". The role of human resources in any organisation is critical in the sense that different people have different perceptions, and expectations and all of them have to be properly managed and developed form the organisations success point of view.

If manpower utilises optimumly the State and Central Governments grows rapidly. In India agriculture is a leading sector and provides jobs to millions and so needs scientific training and temper. Education and health are to be spreaded vehemently and compulsorily to all. Profit, efficiency and production are inter-dependent.

The study of human resources development (HRD) in India is vital from the point of view of economic welfare. Though the HRD is known throughout the ages, its re-discovery as an essential element in development is necessitated by deteriorating social conditions, increased competition and rapid technological advancements. HRD is emerging out as version of 'corporate branding' by which the companies can establish an image of their products and services amongst customers in a fast growing competitive environment which will help in retaining and motivating employees. The competitiveness that is existing today clearly speaks that time has come to reposition and rethink the role of human resources and to focus on division of labour, capability of dexterity, skill development. The purpose of HRD is to help people to lead a fuller and rich life and to unlock the doors to modernization.

Significance of HRD

If India wants to go "global" and to grow "global" due importance should be given to HR. A company is known by the people it keeps. In today's global, decentralized, information driven economy, knowledge has been recognized as a valuable intangible resource that contributes to the success of the firm. 'Retaining' the talented employees is more important that acquiring new blood. But retaining is extremely difficult nowadays and retention war becomes worse in the times to come. The focus should be to give a meaning to employees regarding their role.

Mentoring : The Latest HR Mantra

Employees are the brand image of any company. The companies aspiring expansion plans, pay ever increasing salaries and go for employee motivation and retention plans with proper mentoring. Mentoring traces back its origin to *Mahabharata* times when Lord Krishna enlightened Arjuna of his duties showing true virtues of a friend, guide and *guru*. Therefore organisation can use the art of mentoring as a tool to help ensure 'bringing the best' in an employee for their synergistic growth and success. Encouraging the institution of mentorship will positively influence employees commitment, contribution and continuity. Human resources are the fundamental reason for the success of any knowledge industry company. Therefore organisations wanting successfulness must possess ability to leverage human potential to deliver best business results.

Feature of Human Resources

There is growing awareness that individual development is key to organization development. By virtue that labour is human and living and inseparable from laborers, highly perishable and the fast changing business world, realized the view that human resources are the most important and the HRD is the key factor for enhancing the process, the groups were given freedom to work at their own pace and teachers served as advisors. This resulted in better classroom performance and enhanced the ability to grasp the subject and boost the confidence level of the students.

The success of HRD to a large extent depends upon the existence of a favorable HRD climate. HRD is more personnel - oriented than technology oriented and believes that participation and communication would being about greater commitment, efficiency and growth of individuals.

Different states have promulgated labour legislation regulating and promoting labour process. Labour is considered as an asset both to person and state. Human resource is considered as both cause and effect of economic development. Human resource consists of total skills, creative abilities, talents and aptitudes of an organisational work force, as well as values, beliefs, trust, team spirit, participation, fair compensation, counseling, problem solving valuing the assets and respect for the individual etc. Labour is transformed into human capital. Recent studies have focused on two main ways of human capital management practice that might enhance performance.

- Through raising skills base of employees and ability to use their skills through measures such as design system, participative problem solving and team work.
- Though enhancing employee motivation and ability to use their skills through measures such as design system, participative problem solving and team work.

HRD Model

Managing people is an art and essence of being manager knowledge and skills are required to manage the new challenges due to deregulation and introduction of international standards in some service sectors. All the above changes call for a new orientation in human resource management and development. The quality of human resource is not doubt a critical feature in the success of any sector. Manpower management is undoubtedly the most important and most sensitive and critical area of management that needs to be handled with utmost care and diligence.

The HRM model must focus the promotion of human activity for positive change. The set of activities that can be followed by any organization may include training and development, organizing and development, job development, Human resource planning selection and staffing, personal research and information systems, compensation benefits, employee assistance, labour relations and unions.

Liberalisation has opened up several opportunities for organisational growth as well as personal growth. The human resource development policies must aim at integrating personal development policies must aim at integrating personal development of individual with that of organisation plan so that both organisation and individuals gain from the excuse. The need of the hour is to align the human resources to the organisational needs and strategies. Todays market situation, besides the skill development call for change in the mindset, attitude and behavior of the employees. Therefore sufficient provision should be made before adopting new strategies to bring about the required change in mindset and attitude in the employees and creating knowledge workers to align with organizations goal.

Employee Assistance Programme (EAP) and HRD

The EAPs are designed to look after the well being of " Human Assets". EAPs have been a frequent source to support of employees in personal flux and organizational crisis. Therefore proper EAPs should be defined taking the fact into account the organizational and individual development.

The Human Resource (HR) department should develop systems and process so that ideas are continuously generated and reach the top management. Today HR department is taking a major turn in the competitive environment of knowledge to living organization, *i.e.*, HR department is adding immense value to the business and playing vital elite role in the overall business strategy.

Corporate Culture

The intention of creating corporate culture is to provide a climate and ambience of mutual trust, within which all employees in that company can decide to grow and develop to their full potential. Besides this corporate culture that not only fits into the decision and rationale of the work practices of an organization, but also meets the character and capabilities of a large and diverse work force. Corporate culture crating process also helps in achieving "organizational goals" instead of "individual goals" through covering all employees and not look with myopic and single issue.

Corporate culture creating revolves around group of employees instead of individual charisma. Another important feature of creating corporate culture is that it helps to shape the group leader ship. It is the managers responsibility to create a kind of physical and psychological environment essential to secure the co operation of every employee which indeed a Herculean task, it aims in developing trust among employees.

HRD in Service Organizations

Banking and insurance organizations basically consisting of the people, by the people and for the people. Hence the need and importance of human element in the above two organizations can never be ignored. The sudden change in the banking environment made the work force off-guard and for a pretty long time banks remained direction less. The same tendency also applies to the insurance, transportation and other service organizations. Therefore it is necessary in every bank to analyze their human resource strategies on the basis of SWOT analysis. They must analyze their strengths, weakness, opportunities and threats. Training is an integral part of human resource development. With the liberalization of the economy and the financial sector, the training system in banks should be refined and made to address new frontiers like :

(*i*) Product development and marketing.

(*ii*) Modern credit management skills,

(*iii*) New risks management practices,

(*iv*) Skills for operations in electronic environment, and

(*v*) Bringing about a new focus on the customer and his needs.

HRD and Education

Human capital and social capital are highly invaluable assets to any organization, in particular and nation, in general. Value based qualitative education form bottom to the top including research could bring umpteen achievement to people, institutions and democracy. Lower student and teacher ratio definitely, adds value to the education system which will later reflect on employer employee harmonious growth. If India wanted to "go global" and to "grow global" quality of education and training institutions for every disciplines like farming, manufacturing, service sectors are to be established and given stringent training at least once in two years. Genuine research and development programs are to be initiated and financed by both state and private secor.

HRD and Manpower in Rural Non-farm Sector

In rural India there is more under unemployment and unemployment even after green blue and white revolutions. Though agriculture is providing jobs to millions in our country, it alone cannot sustain the growing population in villages. Therefore it is imperative that rural non-farm sector is to be strengthened. According to the National Sample Survey, the percentage of employment increased from 18.4 per cent in 1983, to 21.6 per cent in 1993-94 and 23.8 per cent in 1999-2000. Poor quality of employment and incomes, shortage of skilled labour, non-availability of credit facilities, absence of marketing networks, poor transporting facilities, low public investments in villages. Rural industrialisation should not come in the form of charity.

HRD and Health-Care Services to People

In order to improve the efficiency of the employees, health development is to be given to p priority. Higher the standard of health higher is the contribution for promotion of enterprise growth and development. Government alone cannot take up all quantitative and qualitative health care facilities in rural side, wherein the farmer and allied communities would benefit and promote production and productivity. The health department can do the monitoring and change the policies and programmers and any additions and deletions. Corporate hospitals are to be directed to extend their branches at rural level, to serve the farming community, in general, farm labour, in particular.

Conclusion

Since HR department offer expertise in creating, implementing, managing initiatives for developing and retaining employees and aligning these initiatives with the organizations strategic direction, HR department should be established which can take care of corporate success and customer satisfaction. Since labour is highly perishable it needs constant training for up gradation of information. If manpower utilizes optimumly the state and central government grows rapidly. In India agriculture is a leading sector and provides jobs to millions and so needs scientific training and temper. Education and health are to be spreaded vehemently and compulsorily to all. Profit, efficiency and production are interdependent.

Expansion and Reforms in Higher Education in India after Globalisation

—Dr. P. Venkateswarlu*
—Dr. R.N. Misra**

Higher education has made a significant contribution to economic development, social progress and political democracy in independent India. But there is serious cause for concern at this juncture. The proportion of our population, in the relevant age group, that enters the world of higher education is about seven per cent. The opportunities for higher education in terms of the number of places in universities are simply not adequate in relation to our needs. Large segments of our population just do not have access to higher education. What is more, the quality of higher education in most of our universities leaves much to be desired.

At the outset, we would also like to stress that foundations are critical. We believe that an emphasis on expansion and reform of our school system is necessary to ensure that every child has an equal opportunity to enter the world of higher education. We are engaged in consultations on school education. We will send our recommendations in this crucial area in due course. In this letter, we focus on higher education.

The NKC has engaged in formal and informal consultations on this subject with a wide range of people in

* Asst. Prof. in Commerce and Management Studies, Andhra University, Visakhapatnam, A.P.

** Professor of MBA, S.M.I.T., Berhampur, Orissa.

the world of higher education. In addition, we consulted concerned people in parliament, government, civil society and industry. The concerns about the higher education system are widely shared. There was a clear, almost unanimous, view that higher education needs a systematic overhaul, so that we can educate much larger numbers without diluting academic standards. Indeed, this is essential because the transformation of economy and society in the twenty-first century would depend, in significant part, on the spread and the quality of education among our people, particularly in the sphere of higher education. And it is only an inclusive society mat can provide the foundations for a knowledge society.

The objectives of reform and change in our higher education system, as you have often stressed, must be expansion, excellence and inclusion. We recognize that meaningful reform of the higher education system, with a long-term perspective, is both complex and difficult. Yet, it is imperative. Our analysis, diagnosis and prescriptions are set out in a detailed note on higher education which is attached. In this letter, we simply highlight our prescriptions.

Expansion

Create many more universities

The higher education system needs a massive expansion of opportunities, to around 1500 universities nationwide, that would enable India to attain a gross enrolment ratio of at least 15 per cent by 2015. The focus would have to be on new universities, but some clusters of affiliated colleges could also become universities. Such expansion would require major changes in the structure of regulation.

Change the system of regulation for higher education

The present regulatory system in higher education is flawed in some important respects. The barriers to entry are too high. The system of authorising entry is cumbersome. There is a multiplicity of regulatory agencies where mandates are both confusing and overlapping. The system, as a whole, is over-regulated but under-governed. We believe that there is a clear need to establish an Independent Regulatory Authority for Higher Education (IRAHE). The IRAHE must be at an arm's - length from the government and independent of all stakeholders including the concerned Ministries of the Government, along the lines specified below :

- The IRAHE would have to be established by an Act of Parliament, and would be responsible for setting the criteria and deciding on entry.
- It would be the only agency that would be authorized to accord degree granting power to higher education institutions.
- It would be responsible for monitoring standards and settling disputes.
- It would apply exactly the same norms to public and private institutions, just as it would apply the same norms to domestic and international institutions.
- It would be the authority for licensing accreditation agencies.
- The role of the UGC would be re-defined to focus on the disbursement of grants to, and maintenance of, public institutions in higher education. The entry regulatory functions of the AICTE, the MCI and the BCI would be performed by the IRAHE, so that their role would be limited to that of professional associations.

Increase public spending and diversify sources of financing

The expansion of our system of higher education is not possible without enhanced levels of financing. This must necessarily come from both public and private sources:

- Since government financing will remain the cornerstone, government support for higher education should increase to at least 1.5 per cent of GDP, out of a total of at least 6 per cent of GDP for education.

- Even this would not suffice for the massive expansion in higher education that is an imperative. It is essential to explore other possibilities that can complement the increase in public expenditure.
- Most public universities are sitting on a large reservoir of untapped resources in the form of land. It should be possible to draw up norms and parameters for universities to use their available land as a source of finance.
- It is for universities to decide the level of fees but, as a norm, fees should meet at least 20 per cent of the total expenditure in universities. This should be subject to two conditions: first, needy students should be provided with a fee waiver plus scholarships to meet their costs; second, universities should not be penalized by the UGC for the resources raised from higher fees through matching deductions from their grants-in-aid.
- We should nurture the tradition of philanthropic contributions through changes in incentives for universities and for donors. At present, there is an implicit disincentive in both tax laws and trust laws. These laws should be changed so that universities can invest in financial instruments of their choice and use the income from their endowments to build up a corpus.
- Universities should also seek to tap other sources such as alumni contributions and licensing fees. We need to create supportive institutional mechanisms that allow universities to engage professional firms for this purpose.
- It is essential to stimulate private investment in education as a means of extending educational opportunities. It may be possible to leverage public resources, especially in the form of land grants, to attract more (not-for-profit) private investment.

Establish 50 National Universities

We recommend the creation of 50 National Universities that can provide education of the highest standard. As exemplars for the rest of the nation, these universities shall train students in a variety of disciplines, including humanities, social sciences, basic sciences, commerce and professional subjects, at both the undergraduate and post-graduate levels. The number 50 is a long term objective. In the short run, it is important to begin with at least 10 such universities in the next 3 years. National Universities can be established in two ways, by the government, or by a private sponsoring body that sets up a Society, Charitable Trust or Company.

Since public finance is an integral constituent of universities worldwide, most of the new universities shall need significant initial financial support from the government. Each university may be endowed with a substantial *allocation of public land,* in excess of its spatial requirements. The excess land can be a subsequent source of income generation. Exceptions need to be made in existing income tax laws to encourage large endowments. Further, there should be no restriction on the utilization of income in any given period or in the use of appropriate financial instruments. And these universities should have the autonomy to set student fee levels and tap other sources for generating funds.

The National Universities we propose shall admit students on an all-India basis. They shall adopt the principle *of needs-blind admissions.* This will require an extensive system of scholarships for needy students. Undergraduate degrees in the National Universities, in a three-year programme, should be granted on the basis of completing a requisite number of credits, obtained from different courses. The academic year shall therefore be semester-based and students shall be internally evaluated at the end of each course. Transfer of credits from one National University to another shall also be possible. An appropriate system of appointments and incentives is required to maximize the productivity of faculty in these National Universities. Strong linkages shall be forged between teaching and research, universities and industry, and universities and research laboratories. The National Universities shall be department-based and shall not have any affiliated colleges.

Excellence

Reform existing universities

Our endeavour to transform higher education must reform existing institutions, where some steps listed below, and explained in the attached note, are essential:

- Universities should be required to revise or restructure curricula at least once in three years.
- Annual examinations, which test memory rather than understanding, should be supplemented with continuous internal assessment which could begin with a weight of 25 per cent in the total to be raised to 50 per cent over a stipulated period.
- We propose a transition to a course credit system where degrees are granted on the basis of completing a requisite number of credits from different courses, which provides students with choices.
- Universities must become the hub of research once again to capture synergies between teaching and research that enrich each other. This requires not only policy measures but also changes in resource allocation, reward systems and mindsets.
- There must be a conscious effort to attract and retain talented faculty members through better working conditions combined with incentives for performance.
- The criteria for resource allocation to universities should seek to strike a much better balance between providing for salaries or pensions and providing for maintenance, development or investment. It should also recognize the importance of a critical minimum to ensure standards and strategic preferences to promote excellence.

- The elements of infrastructure that support the teaching-learning process, such as libraries, laboratories and connectivity, need to be monitored and upgraded on a regular basis.
- There is an acute need for reform, in the structures of governance of universities that do not preserve autonomy and do not promote accountability. Much needs to be done, but two important points deserve mention. The appointments of Vice-Chancellors must be freed from direct or indirect interventions on the part of governments, for these should be based on search processes and peer judgment alone. The size and composition of University Courts, Academic Councils and Executive Councils, which slow down decision-making processes and sometimes constitute an impediment to change, need to be reconsidered on a priority basis.
- We need, and should strive to create, smaller universities which are responsive to change and easier to manage.

Restructure undergraduate colleges

The system of affiliated colleges for undergraduate education, which may have been appropriate 50 years ago, is no longer adequate or appropriate and needs to be reformed. Indeed, there is an urgent need to restructure the system of undergraduate colleges affiliated to universities.

- The most obvious solution is to provide autonomy to colleges either as individual colleges or as clusters of colleges, on the basis of criteria that have been stipulated in our note. However, this would be able to provide a solution for a limited proportion, or number, of undergraduate colleges.
- Some of these affiliated colleges could be remodelled as community colleges, which could provide both vocational education and formal education.

- A Central Board of Undergraduate Education should be established, along with State Boards of Undergraduate Education, which would set curricula and conduct examinations for undergraduate colleges that choose to be affiliated with them. These Boards would separate the academic functions from the administrative functions and, at the same time, provide quality benchmarks.
- New undergraduate colleges could be established as community colleges, could be affiliated with the Central Board of Undergraduate Education or State Boards of Undergraduate Education, or could be affiliated with some of the new universities that are established.

Promote enhanced quality

The higher education system must provide for accountability to society and create accountability within. An expansion of higher education which provides students with choices and creates competition between institutions is going to be vital in enhancing accountability.

- There should be stringent information disclosure norms for all educational institutions such as their financial situation, physical assets, admissions criteria, faculty positions, academic curricula, as also their source and level of accreditation.
- Evaluation of courses and teachers by students as well as peer evaluation of teachers by teachers should be encouraged.
- There must be 3 focus on upgrading infrastructure, improving the training of teachers and continuous assessment of syllabi and examination systems.
- It is particularly important to enhance the ICT infrastructure. Websites and web-based services would improve transparency and accountability. A portal on higher education and research would

increase interaction and accessibility. A knowledge network would connect all universities and colleges for online open resources.

- It may be necessary to rethink the issue of salary differentials within and between universities along with other means of attracting and retaining talented faculty members. Such salary differentials between and within universities could be effective without being large.
- It is necessary to formulate appropriate policies for the entry of foreign institutions into India and the promotion of Indian institutions abroad, while ensuring a level playing field for foreign and domestic institutions within the country.
- The system of higher education must recognize that there is bound to be diversity and pluralism in any system of higher education, and avoid a uniform one-size-fits-all approach. This sense of pluralism must recognise, rather than ignore or shy away from, such diversity and differentiation.

Conclusion

Ensure access for all deserving students

Education is me fundamental mechanism for social inclusion through the creation of more opportunities. It is, therefore, essential to ensure that no student is denied the opportunity to participate in higher education due to financial constraints. We propose the following measures:

- Institutions of higher education should be encouraged to adopt a *needs blind admissions* policy. This would make it unlawful for educational institutions to take into account any financial factor while deciding whether or not to admit a student
- There must be a well-funded and extensive National Scholarship Scheme targeting economically under-privileged students and students from historically socially disadvantaged groups.

Affirmative action

A major aim of the higher education system must be to ensure that access to education for economically and historically socially underprivileged students is enhanced in a substantially more effective manner:

- Reservations are essential but they are only a part, and one form, of affirmative action.
- Disparities in educational attainments are related to caste and social groups, but are also strongly related to other indicators such as income, gender, region and place of residence. Therefore, we need to develop a meaningful and comprehensive framework that would account for the multi-dimensionality of differences that still persist. For example, a deprivation index could be used to provide weighted scores to students and the cumulative score could be used to supplement a student's school examination score.

Index